CDL Test Study Guide 2015-2016

Table of Contents

Quick Overview

As you draw closer to taking your exam, preparing becomes more and more important. Thankfully, you have this study guide to help you get ready. Use this guide to help keep your studying on track and refer to it often.

This study guide contains several key sections that will help you be successful on your exam. The guide contains tips for what you should do the night before and the day of the test. Also included are test-taking tips. Knowing the right information is not always enough. Many well-prepared test takers struggle with exams. These tips will help equip you to accurately read, assess, and answer test questions.

A large part of the guide is devoted to showing you what content to expect on the exam and to helping you better understand that content. Near the end of this guide is a practice test so that you can see how well you have grasped the content. Then, answers explanations are provided so that you can understand why you missed certain questions.

Don't try to cram the night before you take your exam. This is not a wise strategy for a few reasons. First, your retention of the information will be low. Your time would be better used by reviewing information you already know rather than trying to learn lots of new information. Second, you will likely become stressed as you try to gain large amount of knowledge in a short amount of time. Third, you will be depriving yourself of sleep. So be sure to go to bed at a reasonable time the night before. Being well-rested helps you focus and remain calm.

Be sure to eat a substantial breakfast the morning of the exam. If you are taking the exam in the afternoon, be sure to have a good lunch as well. Being hungry is distracting and can make it difficult to focus. You have hopefully spent lots of time preparing for the exam. Don't let an empty stomach get in the way of success!

When travelling to the testing center, leave earlier than needed. That way, you have a buffer in case you experience any delays. This will help you remain calm and will keep you from missing your appointment time at the testing center.

Be sure to pace yourself during the exam. Don't try to rush through the exam. There is no need to risk performing poorly on the exam just so you can leave the testing center early. Allow yourself to use all of the allotted time if needed.

Remain positive while taking the exam even if you feel like you are performing poorly. Thinking about the content you should have mastered will not help you perform better on the exam.

Once the exam is complete, take some time to relax. Even if you feel that you need to take the exam again, you will be well served by some down time before you begin studying again. It's often easier to convince yourself to study if you know that it will come with a reward!

Test-Taking Strategies

1. Predicting the Answer

When you feel confident in your preparation for a multiple-choice test, try predicting the answer before reading the answer choices. This is especially useful on questions that test objective factual knowledge or that ask you to fill in a blank. By predicting the answer before reading the available choices, you eliminate the possibility that you will be distracted or led astray by an incorrect answer choice. You will feel much more confident in your selection if you read the question, predict the answer, and then find your prediction among the answer choices. After using this strategy, be sure to still read all of the answer choices carefully and completely. If you feel unprepared, you should not attempt to predict the answers. This would be a waste of time and an opportunity for your mind to wander in the wrong direction.

2. Reading the Whole Question

Too often, test takers scan a multiple-choice question, recognize a few familiar words, and immediately jump to the answer choices. Test authors are aware of this common impatience, and they will sometimes prey upon it. For instance, a test author might subtly turn the question into a negative, or he or she might redirect the focus of the question right at the end. The only way to avoid falling into these traps is to read the entirety of the question carefully before reading the answer choices.

3. Looking for Wrong Answers

Long and complicated multiple-choice questions can be intimidating. One way to simplify a difficult multiple-choice question is to eliminate all of the answer choices that are clearly wrong. In most sets of answers, there will be at least one selection that can be dismissed right away. If the test is administered on paper, the test taker could draw a line through it to indicate that it may be ignored; otherwise, the test taker will have to perform this operation mentally or on scratch paper. In either case, once the obviously incorrect answers have been eliminated, the remaining choices may be considered. Sometimes identifying the clearly wrong answers will give the test taker some information about the correct answer. For instance, if one of the remaining answer choices is a direct opposite of one of the eliminated answer choices, it may well be the correct answer. The opposite of obviously wrong is obviously right! Of course, this is not always the case. Some answers are obviously incorrect simply because they are irrelevant to the question being asked. Still, identifying and eliminating some incorrect answer choices is a good way to simplify a multiple-choice question.

4. Don't Overanalyze

Anxious test takers often overanalyze questions. When you are nervous, your brain will often run wild causing you to make associations and discover clues that don't actually exist. If you feel that this may be a problem for you, do whatever you can to slow down during the test. Try taking a deep breath or counting to ten. As you read and consider the question, restrict yourself to the particular words used by the author. Avoid thought tangents about what the author *really* meant, or what he or she was *trying* to say. The only things that matter on a multiple-choice test are the words that are actually in the question. You must avoid reading too much into a multiple-choice question, or supposing that the writer meant something other than what he or she wrote.

5. No Need for Panic

It is wise to learn as many strategies as possible before taking a multiple-choice test, but it is likely that you will come across a few questions for which you simply don't know the answer. In this situation, avoid panicking. Because most multiple-choice tests include dozens of questions, the relative value of a single wrong answer is small. Moreover, your failure on one question has no effect on your success elsewhere on the test. As much as possible, you should compartmentalize each question on a multiple-choice test. In other words, you should not allow your feelings about one question to affect your success on the others. When you find a question that you either don't understand or don't know how to answer, just take a deep breath and do your best. Read the entire question slowly and carefully. Try rephrasing the question a couple of different ways. Then, read all of the answer choices carefully. After eliminating obviously wrong answers, make a selection and move on to the next question.

6. Confusing Answer Choices

When working on a difficult multiple-choice question, there may be a tendency to focus on the answer choices that are the easiest to understand. Many people, whether consciously or not, gravitate to the answer choices that require the least concentration, knowledge, and memory. This is a mistake. When you come across an answer choice that is confusing, you need to give it extra attention. A question might be confusing because you do not know the subject matter to which it refers. If this is the case, don't eliminate the answer before you have affirmatively settled on another. When you come across an answer choice of this type, set it aside as you look at the remaining choices. If you can confidently assert that one of the other choices is correct, you can leave the confusing answer aside. Otherwise, you will need to take a moment to try to better understand the confusing answer choice. Rephrasing is one way to tease out the sense of a confusing answer choice.

7. Your First Instinct

Many people struggle with multiple-choice tests because they overthink the questions. If you have studied sufficiently for the test, you should be prepared to trust your first instinct once you have carefully and completely read the question and all of the answer choices. There is a great deal of research to suggest that the mind can come to the correct conclusion very quickly once it has obtained all of the relevant information. At times, it may seem to you as if your intuition is working faster even than your reasoning mind. This may in fact be true. The knowledge you obtain while studying may be retrieved from your subconscious before you have a chance to work out the associations that support it. Verify your instinct by working out the reasons that it should be trusted.

8. Key Words

Many test takers struggle with multiple-choice questions because they have poor reading comprehension skills. Quickly reading and understanding a multiple-choice question requires a mixture of skill and experience. To help with this, try jotting down a few key words and phrases on a piece of scrap paper. Doing this concentrates the process of reading and forces the mind to weigh the relative importance of the question's parts. In selecting words and phrases to write down, the test taker thinks about the question more deeply and carefully. This is especially true for multiple-choice questions that are preceded by a long prompt.

9. Subtle Negatives

One of the oldest tricks in the multiple-choice test writer's book is to subtly reverse the meaning of a question with a word like *not* or *except*. If you are not paying attention to each word in the question, you can easily be led astray by this trick. For instance, a common question format is, "Which of the following is…?" Obviously, if the question instead is, "Which of the following is not….?," then the answer will be quite different. Even worse, the test makers are aware of the potential for this mistake and will include one answer choice that would be correct if the question were not negated or reversed. A test taker who misses the reversal will find what he or she believes to be a correct answer and will be so confident that he or she will fail to reread the question and discover the original error. The only way to avoid this is to practice a wide variety of multiple-choice questions and to pay close attention to each and every word.

10. Reading Every Answer Choice

It may seem obvious, but you should always read every one of the answer choices! Too many test takers fall into the habit of scanning the question and assuming that they understand the question because they recognize a few key words. From there, they pick the first answer choice that answers the question they believe they have read. Test takers who read all of the answer choices might discover that one of the latter answer choices is actually *more* correct. Moreover, reading all of the answer choices can remind you of facts related to the question that can help you arrive at the correct answer. Sometimes, a misstatement or incorrect detail in one of the latter answer choices will trigger your memory of the subject and will enable you to find the right answer. Failing to read all of the answer choices is like not reading all of the items on a restaurant menu. You might miss out on the perfect choice.

11. Spot the Hedges

One of the keys to success on multiple-choice tests is paying close attention to every word. This is never more true than with words like *almost, most, some*, and *sometimes*. These words are called "hedges", because they indicate that a statement is not totally true or not true in every place and time. An absolute statement will contain no hedges, but in many subjects, like literature and history, the answers are not always straightforward. There are always exceptions to the rules in these subjects. For this reason, you should favor those multiple-choice questions that contain hedging language. The presence of qualifying words indicates that the author is taking special care with his or her words, which is certainly important when composing the right answer. After all, there are many ways to be wrong, but there is only one way to be right! For this reason, it is wise when taking a multiple-choice test to avoid answers that are absolute. An absolute answer is one that says things are either all one way or all another. They often include words like *every, always, best*, and *never*. If you are taking a multiple-choice test in a subject that doesn't lend itself to absolute answers, be on your guard if you see any of these words.

12. Long Answers

In many subject areas, the answers are not simple. As already mentioned, the right answer often requires hedges. Another common feature of the answers to a complex or subjective question are qualifying clauses, which are groups of words that subtly modify the meaning of the sentence. If the question or answer choice describes a rule to which there are exceptions or the subject matter is complicated, ambiguous, or confusing, the correct answer will require many words in order to be expressed clearly and accurately. In essence, you should not be deterred by answer choices that seem excessively long. Oftentimes, the author of the text will not be able to write the correct answer without offering some qualifications and modifications. As a test taker, your job is to read the answer choices thoroughly and completely and to select the one that most accurately and precisely answers the question.

13. Restating to Understand

Sometimes, a question on a multiple-choice test is difficult not because of what it asks but because of how it is written. If this is the case, restate the question or answer choice in different words. This process serves a couple of important purposes. First, it forces you to concentrate on the core of the question. In order to rephrase the question accurately, you have to understand it well. Rephrasing the question will concentrate your mind on the key words and ideas. Second, it will present the information to your mind in a fresh way. This process may trigger your memory of some useful scrap of information picked up while studying.

14. True Statements

Sometimes an answer choice will be true in itself, but it does not answer the question. This is one of the main reasons why it is essential to read the question carefully and completely before proceeding to the answer choices. Too often, test takers skip ahead to the answer choices and look for true statements. Having found one of these, they are content to select it without reference to the question above. Obviously, this provides an easy way for test makers to play tricks. The savvy test taker will always read the entire question before turning to the answer choices. Then, having settled on a correct answer choice, he or she will refer to the original question and ensure that the selected answer is relevant. The mistake of choosing a correct-but-irrelevant answer choice is especially common on questions related to specific pieces of objective knowledge, like historical or scientific facts. A prepared test taker will have a wealth of factual knowledge at his or her disposal, but may be careless in its application.

15. No Patterns

One of the more dangerous ideas that circulate about multiple-choice tests is that the correct answers tend to fall into patterns. These erroneous ideas range from a belief that B and C are the most common right answers, to the idea that an unprepared test-taker should answer "A-B-A-C-A-D-A-B-A." It cannot be emphasized enough that pattern-seeking of this type is exactly the WRONG way to approach a multiple-choice test. To begin with, it is highly unlikely that the test maker will plot the correct answers according to some predetermined pattern. The questions are scrambled and delivered in a random order. Furthermore, even if the test maker was following a pattern in the assignation of correct answers, there is no reason why the test maker would know which pattern he or she was using. Any attempt to discern a pattern in the answer choices is a waste of time and a distraction from the real work of taking the test. A test taker would be much better served by extra preparation before the test than by reliance on a pattern in the answers.

General Information

Most states will use a multiple choice CDL test format. This means you will be given a question followed by several possible answers. Usually there will be three to four choices. You are to choose one answer and mark the appropriate selection. This is for the written test only. There will also be a practical (driving) test that will accompany your written test scores. Some states will have laws specific to their state regarding CDL acquisition. Check with your state to find out any state specific laws that they may have. You can usually find this information on your state's DMV or DPS website. This manual does NOT provide information on all the federal and state requirements needed before you can drive a commercial motor vehicle (CMV). Information on CMV operation requirements may be obtained from your state's department of transportation, or the Federal Motor Carrier Safety Administration (FMCSA).

Getting your CDL

When you apply for your CDL, you must show proof of your identity, social security number and residency. You must also provide your most recent medical examiner's certificate. You are required to hold a CDL instruction permit a minimum of 30 days or show successful completion of a DMV or Department of Education approved CDL driver education course. If you already have a driver's license, you can use it as proof of your identity, social security number (dependent on state), and residency. If you do not have a driver's license, you generally must provide the following:

- 2 proof of identity documents, such as a driver's license, birth certificate, government issued photo identification card, CDL instruction permit, unexpired U.S. military identification card or U.S. military discharge papers. You must provide original or duplicate documents. Photocopies will not be accepted.
- 1 proof of your social security number, such as your social security card, IRS W-2 form, payroll check or check stub, unexpired U.S. Military identification card. Photocopies will not be accepted. If you do not want your social security number to be displayed on your license, DMV will issue a control number for your use.
- 1 proof of residency, such as a payroll check or check stub, voter registration card, IRS W-2 form, U.S. or state income tax return. Residency documents must show your name and the address of your principal residence in as it appears on your application for license.

If you are required to meet FMCSA regulations, you must provide your most recent medical examiner's certificate. Medical forms are available at any DMV or DPS office. All drivers must certify that they are in compliance with the Federal Motor Carrier Safety Administration regulations, or that they do not have to comply with them. Refer to the FMCSA regulations for an explanation of these safety requirements.

Vision standards

To operate commercial motor vehicles, you must have:
- 20/40 or better vision in each eye, and
- 140 degrees or better horizontal vision.

These visual requirements must be met without the aid of a telescopic lens. Some drivers may be granted waivers from these vision requirements. For information concerning waivers for travel intra-state, contact your local DMV or DPS. For information concerning waivers for travel inter-state, contact the Federal Motor Carrier Safety Administration at:

Federal Vision & Diabetes Exemptions, MC-PSP Division 400 Seventh Street SW, Room 8301 Washington, DC 20590-0001.

Commercial motor vehicle

A commercial motor vehicle is:
- a single vehicle with a gross vehicle weight rating (GVWR) of 26,001 pounds or more
- a combination of vehicles with a gross combination weight rating of 26,001 pounds or more if the vehicle(s) being towed has a GVWR of more than 10,000 pounds
- vehicles that carry 16 or more passengers, including the driver
- any size vehicle that transports hazardous materials and that requires federal placarding.

Commercial drivers

Commercial drivers refer to anyone that operates commercial motor vehicles in a paid or volunteer position. Mechanics who test drive commercial vehicles must also meet commercial driver's license requirements. Commercial driver's license requirements do not apply to the following:
- emergency vehicle operators, such as EMS or firefighters
- active duty military personnel operating military vehicles
- operators of farm vehicles when
  - operated by farmers
  - used to move farm goods, supplies or machinery to or from their farm
  - not used as a common or contract motor carrier, and
  - used within 150 miles of the farm
- vehicles operated by persons only for personal use, such as recreational vehicles and moving van rentals.

CDL age requirements

You must be at least 18 years of age to hold a CDL. Under federal law, you must be a commercial driver at least 21 years of age to drive across state lines, transport hazardous materials or transport interstate freight within the state. Your license will have an indication that you are restricted to intrastate driving.

CDL instruction permit

The first step in obtaining your CDL is obtaining a commercial driver's license instruction permit. It is similar to a learner's permit you may have had as a teenager. To obtain a CDL instruction permit, you must first pass a CDL general knowledge exam and any other exams for the vehicles that you plan to operate (e.g. Tanker, Passenger, HAZMAT, Triples, Doubles, etc.). Some of these endorsements may also combine to make one endorsement. Once you have been issued your permit, you are only able to use it when accompanied by a fully licensed driver with the same endorsements for which you are training. Often times when you are attending a driving school, there will be multiple permit holders and one fully licensed driver/instructor.

CDL classifications

The classification of what type of CDL you will need is dependent upon the vehicle you plan to operate. To determine which class pertains to you, review the following descriptions. In the following descriptions, GVWR refers to Gross Vehicle Weight Rating, and GCWR refers to Gross Combined Weight Rating.

Class A
Any combination of vehicles with a GCWR of 26,001 pounds or more if the vehicle(s) being towed have a GVWR of more than 10,000 pounds. Vehicles in this class include:
- tractor-trailer
- truck and trailer combinations
- tractor-trailer buses

If you hold a class A CDL and you have all required endorsements, you are also permitted to operate those vehicles listed in classes B and C of this section.

Class B
Any single vehicle with a GVWR of 26,001 pounds or more. Any single vehicle with a GVWR of 26,001 pounds or more towing another vehicle with a GVWR of 10,000 pounds or less. This class includes:
- straight trucks
- large buses
- segmented buses
- trucks towing vehicles with a GVWR of 10,000 pounds or less

If you hold a class B CDL and you have all required endorsements, you are also permitted to operate those vehicles listed in class C of this section.

Class C
Any vehicle that is not included in classes A or B that carries hazardous materials or is designed to carry 16 or more passengers, including the driver.

CDL endorsements

- H: Hazardous Material
- N: Tank Vehicle
- P: Passenger
- S: School bus
- T: Double/Triple Trailer
- X: Combination of N and H (as mentioned in the section on permits)

CDL restrictions

The letter code for restrictions will vary by state and not all states have the same amount of restriction codes. You can find out what your state's CDL restrictions are by contacting your DMV or DPS office via their website, telephone or in-person visit. Please note that in-person visits may take longer due to potential waiting times at your nearest location.

Moving violations

If you receive two or more moving violations within the average 5-year life of your CDL license (driving either a private or commercial vehicle) you must retake all written exams applicable to your CDL license.

Taking the CDL tests

All persons seeking a CDL are required to take a written test as well as a practical (driving) test. All CDL classifications will require a general knowledge exam. You will also need to take a test for transporting cargo. If you are going to operate a vehicle with air brakes, you will need to also take a test specific to their operation. If you choose not to take the air brakes test, there will be a restriction code placed on your CDL indicating that you cannot operate any vehicle with air brakes. If the vehicle you plan to operate is a combination vehicle, you will need to complete the corresponding test. To determine which of these sections you need to focus on for your CDL, refer to the table below.

Class A, B, C	General Knowledge/Transporting Cargo
Air Brake Vehicles	Air Brakes
Class A Combination	Combination Vehicles
T	Doubles and Triples
N	Tanker Vehicles
H	Hazardous Material
P	Passenger
S	School Bus
X	Tanker Vehicles/Hazardous Material

There will be a fee to take your exams. The frequency of how often you can test for your written exams will vary by state. Some states may also have a retest fee. You can find out any testing fees and retest information by contacting your state DMV or DPS office.

The general knowledge exam will determine how familiar you are with operation commercial vehicles. You will see things similar to your first driving exam (e.g. street signs, lights, etc.). You will also encounter specific CDL questions. Using the information you learn from this guide and any experiences from a training program, try to select the best answer. Once you pass the required written exam(s), you can take the skills exams that test your practical knowledge of what you have studied. These exams include three areas:
- pre-trip inspection (be thorough)
- air brakes (if applicable)
- on-road driving (control, shifting, turns)

You must take the skills exams in the type of vehicle for which you want to be licensed. Skills exams are not necessary for all additional endorsements, but are for some. You will need to check with your DPS office prior to testing whether or not your endorsement will require a skills test.

Tip: When backing for your test, (GOAL) Get Out And Look before you back.

Disqualifications

If you are convicted of any of the following violations while operating a commercial motor vehicle, you will be disqualified or prohibited from driving commercial motor vehicles in the future. You will lose your CDL for at least one year for a first offense for:

- Driving a CMV if your breath or blood alcohol concentration is 0.04 or higher.
- Driving your personal vehicle or CMV under the influence of alcohol or a controlled substance.
- Refusing to undergo breath or blood alcohol testing whether in CMV or in personal vehicle.
- Leaving the scene of an accident
- Committing a felony involving the use of a motor vehicle.
- Driving a CMV when the CDL is suspended, revoked, cancelled, or disqualified.
- receive a second conviction for one of the violations listed above; or,
- Causing a fatality through negligent operation of a CMV.
- Driving a CMV in possession of a controlled substance.

You will lose your CDL for at least three years if the offense occurs while you are operating a CMV that is placarded for hazardous materials. You will lose your CDL for life for a second offense, or if you use a CMV to commit a felony involving controlled substances. You will be out-of-service for 24 hours or more if any trace amount of BAC is found less than 0.04. As you may have noticed, the limitations for CDL holders are much stricter than those that operate normal cars and trucks.

Serious violations

Serious traffic violations are speeding 15 mph or more above the posted limit, reckless driving, erratic lane changes, following a vehicle too closely, traffic offenses involving fatal or injury producing traffic accidents, driving without a CDL or having a CDL in the driver's possession, and driving a CMV without the proper classification of CDL or endorsements. There are many more violations for those transporting hazardous materials. These will be explained in the hazardous material section. If you operate a vehicle on some state's roadways, you agree to take a chemical test upon request to determine if you are driving under the influence of alcohol or drugs. This is called implied consent.

General Knowledge

Inspection of vehicle

Safety is a vital reason to perform inspections on your vehicle. Inspecting your vehicle thoroughly for any mechanical problems can prevent breakdowns or accidents. Pre-trip inspections are required by both federal and state laws. Federal and state inspectors can inspect your vehicle at anytime without your permission. The consent is implied when you obtain your CDL. If they find your vehicle to be unsafe, they can put you out of service until the problems have been repaired. If you are convicted of violating an out-of-service order, your CDL may be suspended or revoked. There are three kinds of inspections:

- pre-trip (before operating the vehicle)
- during the trip (watching gauges, mirrors and at each stop)
- post-trip (when you have completed your driving for the day)

Things to watch for during your trip:

- Tires, wheels and rims (check chains in snow travel)
- Brakes (can become overheated in mountain descent)
- Lights and reflectors (make sure all lights are functioning properly)
- Brake and electrical connections to the trailer
- Trailer coupling devices (check the seal on the couplings)
- Cargo covers and tiedowns (make sure hooks are secure during travel)

It's a good idea to inspect your vehicle within the first 25 miles of the trip and also every 150 miles or every 3 hours.

> *Tip: If your couplings aren't sealing well, moisten the connections. Also make sure there is always enough grease on your 5th wheel to ensure a solid trailer connection.*

Inspect your vehicle at the end of your day. If you find any problems with your rig, report them to your dispatcher. They will usually try to find local assistance for you as soon as possible. Make note of things that could be potential issues in the future that you may need to discuss with a mechanic at your company's local yard or truck stop.

<u>What to look for</u>

- Check for proper tire pressure using an air pressure gauge or by hitting them with a mallet. (you are feeling for bounce back from the mallet strike) Look for:
  - Mismatched tire sizes
  - Cuts or other damage to the tires
  - Dual tires touching
- Damaged rims or wheels
- Damage, looseness or rust to lug nuts
- Missing clamps or spacers
- Bent or cracked lock rings

Brakes: Look for brake drum and shoe problems on front, rear and trailer brakes:

- Cracked drums
- Shoes or pads with oil, grease or brake fluid on them
- Shoes worn thin, missing or broken

Steering system

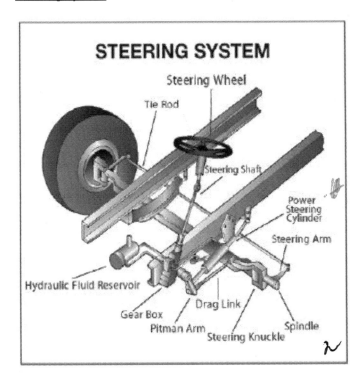

Look for:
- Missing nuts, bolts, cotter keys or other parts on the steering box
- Bent, loose, or broken parts, such as steering column, steering gear box, or tie rods.
- If power steering equipped, check hoses, pumps, and fluid level; check for leaks.
- Steering wheel play of more than 10 degrees (approximately 2 inches movement at the rim of a 20-inch steering wheel) can make it hard to steer.

Suspension system

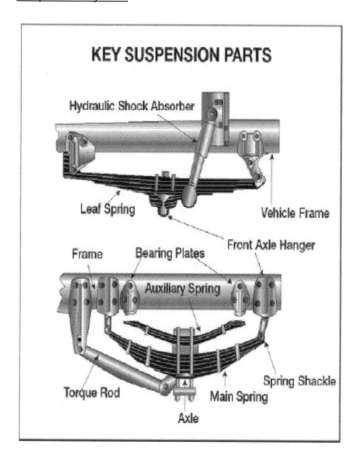

KEY SUSPENSION PARTS

Hydraulic Shock Absorber

Leaf Spring

Vehicle Frame

Front Axle Hanger

Frame

Bearing Plates

Auxiliary Spring

Torque Rod

Main Spring

Spring Shackle

Axle

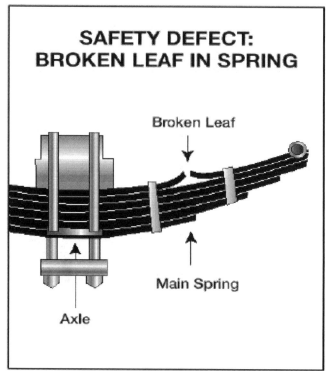

SAFETY DEFECT:
BROKEN LEAF IN SPRING

Broken Leaf

Main Spring

Axle

The suspension system holds up the vehicle and its load. It keeps the axles in place. Therefore, broken suspension parts are very dangerous. Look for front, rear and trailer suspension defects:

- Spring hangers that allow movement of an axle from the proper position
- Cracked or broken spring hangers
- Missing or broken leaves in any leaf spring. If one fourth or more are missing, your vehicle could be put "out of service". But, any defect is dangerous.
- Broken leaves in the multi-leaf spring or leaves that may have shifted to where they are hitting tires or other parts
- Leaking shock absorbers
- Torque rod or arm, u-bolts, spring hangers or other axle positioning parts that are cracked, damaged, or missing
- Air suspension systems that are damaged and or leaking
- Any loose, cracked, broken or missing frame members

Exhaust system defects: Damage to the exhaust system can potentially let poison fumes into the cab or sleeper berth.

- Loose, broken, or missing exhaust pipes, mufflers, tailpipes, or vertical stacks.
- Exhaust system parts rubbing against fuel system parts, tires, or other moving parts of vehicle.
- Loose, broken, or missing mounting brackets, clamps, bolts, or nuts.
- Any leaking parts of the exhaust system.

Emergency equipment

All commercial vehicles must be equipped with emergency equipment including:

- Fire extinguisher(s).
- Spare electrical fuses (unless equipped with circuit breakers).
- Three reflective triangles

Highly recommended equipment for all drivers:

- Tire chains
- Tire changing equipment
- List of emergency phone numbers
- Accident reporting kit (usually provided by employer).

Cargo

Make sure your truck is not overloaded for its rating/permits. Be sure that the cargo is balanced and secured before each trip. Also, if you are using load locks, make sure they are in place before transport. If the cargo contains hazardous materials, make sure you have all proper documents and placards for the load.

Steps for vehicle inspection

Before inspecting your vehicle, make sure that you have set parking brakes and that the wheels are chocked. If you have to tilt the cab (cabover trucks), secure loose items in the cab so they will not fall.

Step 1
Review the last vehicle inspection report. Drivers may have to make a vehicle inspection report each day. The motor carrier must repair any items that affect safety. The motor carrier must certify on the report that the repairs were made or that they were unnecessary.

Step 2

Check the engine compartment:

- Engine oil level
- Coolant level in radiator, condition of hoses
- Power steering fluid level; hose condition (if equipped)
- Windshield washer fluid level
- Battery fluid level, connections and tie downs (battery may be in different location)
- Automatic transmission fluid level (engine must be running)
- Check belts for tightness and wear (alternator, water pump, air compressor)
- Learn how much "give" each belt should have when adjusted right, and then properly check each one.
- Leaks in the engine compartment--fuel, coolant, oil, power steering fluid, hydraulic fluid, battery fluid
- Cracked, worn electrical wiring insulation.

When you have completed this part of your inspection, be sure to lower and secure hood, cab, or engine compartment door. It is very important to make sure the latches are all secure before operation the vehicle.

Step 3

Start the engine and inspect the inside of the cab:

- Get in and start engine
    - Make sure parking brake is set on both truck and trailer (red and yellow knobs), if applicable.
    - Put gearshift in neutral, or park if your transmission provides that option.
    - Start engine and listen for anything abnormal (grinding, whining, etc.).
    - If equipped, check the Anti-lock Braking System (ABS) indicator lights. The light on the dash should turn on and then off. If it stays on, the ABS is malfunctioning and should be reported immediately. For trailers, if the yellow light on the left rear of the trailer stays on, the ABS is not working properly and should also be reported immediately.

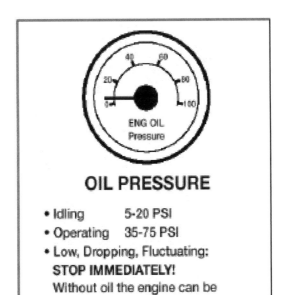

OIL PRESSURE

- Idling   5-20 PSI
- Operating   35-75 PSI
- Low, Dropping, Fluctuating:
  STOP IMMEDIATELY!
  Without oil the engine can be destroyed rapidly

- Check all gauges:
  - Oil pressure will take time to rise but should come up to normal within seconds after the engine is started. Some older models may take longer.
  - Ammeter and/or voltmeter should be in normal range.
  - Coolant temperature. Should begin gradual rise until normal level.
  - Engine oil temperature. Should begin gradual rise until normal level.
  - Warning lights and buzzers should go out right away.
  - Air pressure should build from 50 to 90 psi within a 3 minute time frame. Increasing the RPM will cause air pressure to rise to normal levels (around 120-140 psi)
- Check all controls for looseness, sticking, damage or improper setting.
  - Steering wheel
  - Clutch
  - Accelerator (gas pedal)
  - Brake controls:
  - Foot brake
  - Trailer brake (if applicable)
  - Parking brake
  - Retarder controls (if applicable)
  - Transmission controls
  - Interaxle differential lock (if applicable)
  - Horns (air and normal)
  - Windshield wiper blades and washer function.
  - Lights:
  - Headlights
  - Dimmer switch
  - Turn signals
  - 4-way flashers
  - Clearance, identification, marker light switches
  - Parking lights

- Check all mirrors and windshield. Look for cracks, dirt, illegal stickers or other potential obstructions to your view. Make any necessary adjustments.
- Check all emergency equipment
  - Fully functional fire extinguisher
  - Spare fuses on hand
  - Three reflective triangles and/or road flares
  - Make sure that your safety belt is not frayed or torn and that all latches work properly.
- You will also want to inspect any optional equipment
  - Tire chains (for snowy/icy conditions).
  - Equipment for changing tires if needed.
  - Tire chains (for snowy/icy conditions)

When you have completed all checks inside the cab, turn your engine off and test all of your lights outside of your vehicle. Make sure that your parking brakes are set and your key is removed from the ignition.

Step 4
Make a walk-around inspection:
- Check that all lights are working as mentioned above.
- Check the front left side
  - Driver's door glass
  - Door latches
  - Left front wheel
  - Left front suspension
  - Left front brake
  - Left fuel tanks (check tank straps for wear)
- Front
  - Front axle
  - Steering system
  - Windshield
  - Lights and reflectors
- Front right
  - Front right checks (same areas as front left)
  - Right fuel tanks (check tank straps for wear)
  - Condition of all parts inspected
- Transmission
  - Exhaust system
  - Frame and cross members
  - Air lines and electrical wiring—look for snagging, rubbing, wearing
  - Spare tire carrier or rack
  - Spare tire and/or wheel securely mounted in rack
  - Spare tire and wheel (proper size, properly inflated)
- Cargo securement
  - Cargo properly blocked, braced, tied, chained.
  - Tailboards up and properly secured.
  - End gates free of damage, properly secured in stake sockets.
  - Canvas or tarp (if required) properly secured to prevent tearing, billowing or blocking of either the rearview mirrors or rear lights.
  - If vehicle is oversized, check that all required signs (flags, lamps and reflectors are safely and properly mounted and that you have all required permits
  - Make sure all compartment doors are securely closed, latched or locked and that required security seals are in place.

- Right rear
  - Wheels and rims
  - Tires
  - Suspension
  - Brakes
  - Lights and reflectors
- Rear
  - Lights and reflectors
  - License plate
  - Splash guards
  - Cargo securement
- Left side--Check all items checked for the right side. Also check:
  - Battery(s) if they are not mounted in the engine compartment
- Check all signal lights.

Step 5
Start the engine and check the brake system:
- Hydraulic brakes
  - If the vehicle has hydraulic brakes, pump the brake pedal 3 times.
  - Apply firm pressure to the pedal and hold for 5 seconds.
  - The pedal should not move.
  - If it does, there may be a leak or other problem. This must be fixed immediately.
- Air brakes
  - If the vehicle has air brakes, build air pressure to 100-120 psi. Turn off the engine, release all brakes.
  - Press hard on the foot brake and hold down for one minute.
  - On combination vehicles, air pressure should not drop over 4 psi.
  - On single vehicles, air pressure should not drop over 3 psi.
  - Turn ignition on.
  - With the foot brake, pump the air pressure down. At about 60 psi, the low air buzzer should sound.
  - Keep pumping air down with foot brake. At about 40 psi, the tractor parking brake knob and the trailer parking brake knob should pop out.
- Parking brakes
  - Set the parking brake.
  - Put the vehicle in low gear and gently release the clutch until you feel the tractor pulling against the brake.
  - The vehicle should not move.
- If operating a bus, additional things to check are:
  - the passenger entry
  - seating
  - emergency exits
  - baggage compartment
- If you are driving a tractor trailer, also check:
  - catwalk
  - all parts of the coupling system (5th wheel lower plate, etc.) You will not be able to see the lower plate if the vehicle is hooked up.
  - trailer-front side and rear (air/electrical connections, header board, landing gear, etc.)
  - Make sure the crank handle to your landing gear is secure to avoid any potential hazards from it hanging. Also make sure your gear is lifted all the way.

If you find anything wrong during any step of your inspection, make sure it is fixed before operating your vehicle. It is against federal law to operate an unsafe vehicle. Make sure to wear your safety belt at all times and always watch your mirrors.

During your test, you will be required to point out the areas of the vehicle as instructed and you may even be asked what problems that area could have during an inspection. What is tested varies by state. Key things to focus on for passing your test:

1. Air brake test
2. Pre-trip inspection
3. Use of mirrors
4. Shifting
5. Turning

There are many others that are also of vital importance. These are some of the most important to make sure you know before testing.

Basic Control of Your Vehicle

Skills

To operate any vehicle safely, you must know how to control its speed and direction. This is especially true of CDL drivers because of the size of their vehicles. The following is a list of skills that you will need to understand extremely well before operating your vehicle:
- Accelerating
- Steering
- Shifting gears
- Backing
- Braking
- Constantly checking your mirrors

Ultimately, these skills need to be mastered, not just understood. They will ensure safe driving for you and the motorists around you. Always remember to fasten your seatbelt before operating any vehicle.

Accelerating

Partly engage the clutch before taking your foot off the brake (unless fully automatic). Too little or too much and you will stall. Use the parking brake when on an incline to keep from rolling back. Release it only when you have enough power to keep from rolling back. If you are operating a tractor-trailer with a trailer brake hand valve, you can use it to keep from rolling back. The trailer brakes can be a much safer method if equipped. You want to slowly accelerate to prevent jerking of the vehicle. If not done properly, your truck will stall. If you are pulling a trailer, the jerking can damage the coupling. Make sure to pull slowly and try to feel when the trailer has engaged. These steps are especially important in conditions where traction may be poor, such as in rain, sleet, or snow. If you do not follow these steps in these conditions, the drive wheels will spin, causing you to lose control of the vehicle. If you feel your wheels start to spin, slowly let off of the accelerator until you find traction. With the use of tire chains, chances of your drive tires spinning are decreased.

Steering

Hold the steering wheel with both hands. Your hands should be on opposite sides of the steering wheel. Avoid sharp motions to the steering wheel; this could cause your vehicle to whip due to its length.

Shifting gears

Correct shifting of gears is very important. If you can't get your vehicle into the right gear while driving, you will have less control and may have a more difficult time stopping.

Shifting up
Double clutching is the most common method used by those learning to shift. It is commonly used in truck driving schools. This is the basic method:
- Take your foot off the accelerator. Push in the clutch and shift into neutral.
- Release the clutch
- Let the engine slow down the RPMs required for the next gear (usually 1000 RPMs slower but this can vary from truck to truck.).
- Push in the clutch and shift to the higher gear.
- Let off the clutch and push the accelerator as you would on takeoff.

This method of shifting will take a lot of repetition and practice. You can't stay in neutral too long or you will not be able to engage the next gear. If this happens, speed up your RPMs to engage the next gear. Do not force it. If you can't execute the shift, go back to your original gear and try again.

Shifting down
- Release accelerator, push in clutch, and shift to neutral at the same time.
- Release clutch.
- Press accelerator, increase engine and gear speed to the rpm required in the lower gear.
- Push in clutch and shift to lower gear at the same time.
- Release clutch and press accelerator at the same time.

Pedal operation is very similar for shifting up or down. You just need to know when you need to shift and what the RPMs should be for each shift.

Tip: Shifting down can help when you are having trouble stopping.

Special conditions where you should downshift are:
- Before starting down a hill. Slow down and shift down to a speed that you can control without using the brakes hard. Otherwise the brakes can overheat and lose their braking power.
- Before entering a curve. Slow down to a safe speed, and downshift before you enter the curve. This allows you to use some power through the curve to help the vehicle be more stable while turning. It also allows you to speed up as soon as you are out of the curve.

Backing safely

When operating your vehicle, you are not able to see everything behind you, which makes backing very dangerous. Try to avoid backing whenever possible. When you must back, do so properly. Follow these simple steps:
- Map the path you will follow when backing. Get out and look (GOAL) is very important when backing, during your road test and in everyday driving.
- Turn on four-way flashers and sound your horn before backing to ensure that all bystanders are clear, and to let other vehicles know that you are backing.
- Do not back fast. There is no room for error if you do. Use the lowest reverse gear.
- You always want to driver's side back whenever possible. This means backing with full view of the driver's side of the vehicle. The other way is considered "blind side backing" and can lead to more accidents. Whenever you have no other way, try to find a spotter to aid you when backing.
- Even in driver's side backing, if you have someone that can spot you in backing, utilize them. They can check all of your blind spots for you and signal directions to you. Your spotter should always stand where he or she has a view of the rear of the truck and where the driver can see them. If you lose sight of them during your backing, stop until you know their location. They may be in an area where they could be injured. Before you begin backing, agree on hand signals that you both understand. Audible directions are not always possible given the loud noises of the trucks and loading docks.

Backing with a trailer

When backing vehicles without trailers, you turn the steering wheel in the direction that you want the back of your vehicle to go. When backing with a trailer, you need to turn the steering wheel in the opposite direction. To follow the trailer during your backing, you need to turn in the direction the trailer is going. This will straighten the position of your truck with the trailer. Whenever possible, always try to back in a straight line. If you have no other option and must back on a curved path, always back to the driver's side so you can see the path of your trailer. Remember to back slowly. Always use your mirrors. They help you see if the trailer is staying on the proper path or not. They also make it easier to see when corrections need to be made. Whenever you need to make a correction that cannot be done with small turns of the steering wheel during backing, pull up and realign your truck and trailer with your target. Pull up as often as you need to ensure that you back in properly.

Retarders

Retarders help slow diesel vehicles, reducing the need for using your brakes. They reduce brake wear and give you another way to slow down. There are four types of retarders:
- Exhaust
- Engine
- Hydraulic
- Electric

All retarders can be turned on or off by the driver. The power can also be adjusted on some vehicles. When activated, retarders reduce the engine power once you take your foot off the accelerator completely. If you are pushing the accelerator, it will not reduce power. Do not use your retarders in inclement weather where slippery conditions are present, especially if the unit is empty or lightly loaded. Because these devices can be noisy, some city ordinances do not allow use of them within city limits. You should see signs saying "No Engine Breaks" or something similar.

Mirrors

Use all of your mirrors to check the traffic around you and your vehicle for any problems (flat tires, fire, cargo straps, etc.). Using your mirrors is especially vital when turning, changing lanes, or merging. Do not lose focus on the road ahead. Use your mirrors to check your tires. If you are carrying open cargo, use the mirrors to check that all of your straps or chains are still secure. Also, look for a flapping or ballooning tarp. All of these things are very important to check often. Many vehicles have curved mirrors that show a wider area than flat mirrors to help with blind spots. Everything in a curved mirror appears smaller and farther away than it really is. Make sure you adjust all of your mirrors before each trip as they may have been moved at some point. They are your lifelines.

Planning ahead

Stopping or changing lanes may take a lot of distance. You must know what the traffic is doing at all times from all sides of your vehicle. Experienced drivers plan ahead by looking far in front of them so they can estimate how much room they have to make any necessary moves in traffic. On the highway, most drivers look approximately ¼ of a mile ahead. When you plan ahead, look for traffic, road conditions, sharp pavement drop-offs and signs. Also look for slow-moving vehicles. Be especially careful when driving through work zones or when you see a law enforcement vehicle on the shoulder. Do not focus solely on what is in the distance. You want to scan constantly all around you and in the distance. Once you are accustomed to doing this, it becomes routine.

Communication

Signaling

It is important to let others know what you are doing on the road. You should always use your vehicle to communicate with other drivers. Just as you would with a car, you will use your headlights, turning signals, etc. Signaling what you intend to do is important for safety. Here are some general rules for signaling:

- Signal ahead
  - Signal early
  - Signal before you turn, merge or change lanes.
  - Brake early and slow gradually for turns.
  - Flash your brake lights to warn other drivers that you need to slow down or stop. Don't stop suddenly.
  - Turn off your signal after you make the turn, merge or lane change (not all vehicles' signals turn off automatically after the turn).
  - Use your emergency flashers when moving slowly (less than 45 mph on most freeways) or when you are parked.
  - Do not signal other drivers to pass you. They cannot see around you and it could lead to an accident.
- Always pass with caution
  - Check your side mirrors for surrounding traffic.
  - Determine if you have sufficient room to pass.
  - Use your turn signal early so that vehicles from behind know of your intentions.
  - Always check the surrounding traffic again before beginning your pass.
- Communicate your presence to others
  - Whenever you are about to pass a vehicle, pedestrian, or bicyclist, assume they don't see you.
  - Drive carefully enough to avoid a crash even if they don't see or hear you.
  - At dawn, dusk, in rain, or snow, you need to make yourself easier to see.
  - Turn on your lights. Use the headlights, not just the identification or clearance lights.
  - Use the low beams; high beams can bother people in the daytime as well as at night.
  - Use your horn only when needed. Otherwise, your horn may scare others.

- When you stop on the side of the road:
  - Turn on your 4-way emergency flashers.
  - Place reflective triangles or flares within 10 minutes of stopping.
  - See the following images:

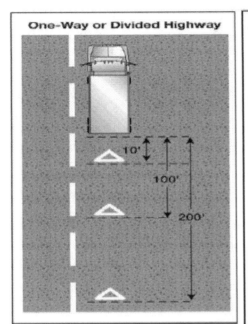

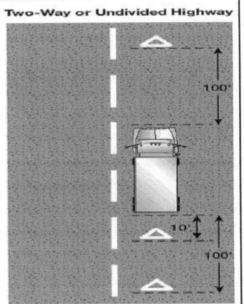

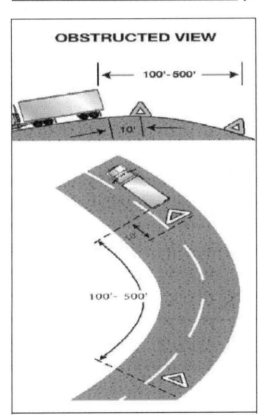

When putting out the triangles, hold them between yourself and the oncoming traffic for your own safety (So other drivers can see you). It could save your life.

Space Management

To be a safe driver, you need space all around your vehicle. When things go wrong, space gives you time to think and to take action. To have space available when something goes wrong, you need to manage space. While this is true for all drivers, it is very important for large vehicles. They take up more space and they require more space for stopping and turning.

Space ahead

You need space ahead in case you must suddenly stop. According to accident reports, the vehicle that trucks and buses most often run into is the one in front of them. The most frequent cause is following too closely. Remember, if the vehicle ahead of you is smaller than yours, it can probably stop faster than you can. You may crash if you are following too closely. One good rule says you need at least one second for each 10 feet of vehicle length at speeds below 40 mph. At greater speeds, you must add 1 second for safety. For example, if you are driving a 40-foot vehicle, you should leave 4 seconds between you and the vehicle ahead. In a 60-foot rig, you'll need 6 seconds. Over 40 mph, you'd need 5 seconds for a 40-foot vehicle and 7 seconds for a 60-foot vehicle. To know how much space you have, wait until the vehicle ahead passes a shadow on the road, a pavement marking, or some other clear landmark. Then count off the seconds like this: "one thousand- and-one, one thousand-and-two" and so on, until you reach the same spot.

Examples:
- If you are driving a 40-foot vehicle at speeds under 40 mph, leave 4 seconds between you and the vehicle ahead. One second for each 10 feet of vehicle length = 1X4 or 4 seconds.
- If you are driving a 40-foot vehicle at speeds over 40 mph, leave 5 seconds between you and the vehicle ahead. One second for each 10 feet of vehicle length plus an additional second for safety: 1X4 = 4 plus an extra second for safety = 5 seconds.
- If you are driving a 60-foot vehicle at speeds under 40 mph, leave 6 seconds between you and the vehicle ahead. One second for each 10 feet of the vehicle length = 1X6 or 6 seconds.
- If you are driving a 60-foot vehicle at speeds over 40 mph, leave 7 seconds between you and the vehicle ahead. One second for each 10 feet of vehicle length plus an additional second for safety: 1X6 = 6 plus an extra second for safety = 7 seconds.

Remember that in inclement weather, these times increase greatly.

Space behind

You can't stop others from following you too closely. But there are things you can do to make it safer:
- Stay to the right. Heavy vehicles are often tailgated when they can't keep up with the speed of traffic. This often happens when you're going uphill. If a heavy load is slowing you down, stay in the right lane if you can. Going uphill, you should not pass another slow vehicle unless you can get around quickly and safely.
- Dealing with tailgaters safely. In a large vehicle, it's often hard to see whether a vehicle is close behind you.
- You may be tailgated:
  - When you are traveling slowly. Drivers trapped behind slow vehicles often follow closely.
  - In bad weather. Many car drivers follow large vehicles closely during bad weather, especially when it is hard to see the road ahead.
- If you find yourself being tailgated, here are some things you can do to reduce the chances of a crash.
- Avoid quick changes. If you have to slow down or turn, signal early, and reduce speed very gradually.
- Increase your following distance. Opening up room in front of you will help you to avoid having to make sudden speed or direction changes. It also makes it easier for the tailgater to get around you.
- Don't speed up. It's safer to be tailgated at a low speed than a high speed.
- Avoid tricks. Don't turn on your taillights or flash your brake lights. Follow the suggestions above.

Space to the sides

Commercial vehicles are often wide and take up most of a lane. Safe drivers will manage what little space they have. You can do this by keeping your vehicle centered in your lane, and avoid driving alongside others. You need to keep your vehicle centered in the lane to keep safe clearance on either side. If your vehicle is wide, you have little room to spare. There are two dangers in traveling alongside other vehicles:
- Another driver may change lanes suddenly and turn into you.
- You may be trapped when you need to change lanes.

Find an open spot where you aren't near other traffic. When traffic is heavy, it may be hard to find an open spot. If you must travel near other vehicles, try to keep as much space as possible between you and them. Also, drop back or pull forward so that you are sure the other driver can see you.

Strong winds
Strong winds make it difficult to stay in your lane. The problem is usually worse for lighter vehicles. This problem can be especially bad coming out of tunnels. Don't drive alongside others if you can avoid it.

Space overhead

Hitting overhead objects is a danger. Make sure you always have overhead clearance.
- Don't assume that the heights posted at bridges and overpasses are correct. Re-paving or packed snow may have reduced the clearances since the heights were posted.
- The weight of a cargo van changes its height. An empty van is higher than a loaded one. That you got under a bridge when you were loaded does not mean that you can do it when you are empty.
- If you doubt you have safe space to pass under an object, go slowly. If you aren't sure you can make it, take another route. Warnings are often posted on low bridges or underpasses, but sometimes they are not.
- Some roads can cause a vehicle to tilt. There can be a problem clearing objects along the edge of the road, such as signs, trees, or bridge supports. Where this is a problem, drive a little closer to the center of the road.
- Before you back into an area, get out and check for overhanging objects such as trees, branches, or electric wires. It's easy to miss seeing them while you are backing. (Also check for other hazards at the same time.)

Space below

Many drivers forget about the space under their vehicles. That space can be very small when a vehicle is heavily loaded. This is often a problem on dirt roads and in unpaved yards. Don't take a chance on getting hung up. Drainage channels across roads can cause the ends of some vehicles to drag. Cross such depressions carefully. Railroad tracks can also cause problems, particularly when pulling trailers with a low underneath clearance. Don't take a chance on getting hung up halfway across.

Space for turns

Because of wide turning and offtracking, large vehicles can hit other vehicles or objects during turns. When turning right:

- Turn slowly to give yourself and others time to avoid problems.
- If you cannot make the right turn without swinging into another lane, turn wide as you complete the turn. Refer to the diagram. Keep the rear of your vehicle close to the curb. This will stop other drivers from passing you on the right.
- Don't turn to the left as you start the turn. The driver behind you may think you are turning left and try to pass you on the right.
- If you must cross into an oncoming lane to make a turn, watch out for vehicles coming toward you. Give them room to pass or stop. However, don't back up for them. You could hit the vehicle behind you.

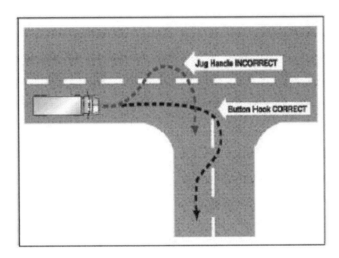

When turning left:

- Reach the center of the intersection before you begin your turn. If you turn too soon, your vehicle could hit another vehicle because of offtracking.
- If there are two lanes, always use the right turn lane. Don't begin a left turn in the left lane because you may have to swing right to complete the turn. You can see drivers on your left easier than those on your right.

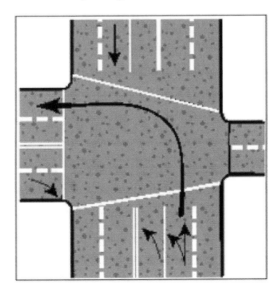

Space to cross or enter traffic

Be aware of the size and weight of your vehicle when you cross or enter traffic.
- Because of slow acceleration and the space large vehicles require, you may need a much larger gap to enter traffic than you would in a car.
- Acceleration varies with your load. Allow more room if your vehicle is fully loaded.
- Before you begin across a road, make sure you can get all the way across before traffic reaches you.

Controlling speed

Driving too fast is a major cause of crashes and fatalities. You must adjust your speed to suit weather conditions, the road (such as hills and curves), visibility and traffic.

Speed and stopping

Three things add up to total stopping distance:

> Perception distance
> Reaction distance
> Braking distance
> = Total stopping distance

- Perception distance is the distance your vehicle travels from the time your eyes see a hazard until your brain recognizes it. Keep in mind certain mental and physical conditions can affect your perception distance. It can be affected greatly depending on visibility and the hazard itself. The average perception time for an alert driver is 1¾ seconds. At 55 mph this accounts for 142 feet traveled.
- Reaction distance is the distance you will continue to travel, in ideal conditions; before you physically hit the brakes, in response to a hazard seen ahead. An average driver has a reaction time of ¾ second to 1 second. At 55 mph this accounts for 61 feet traveled.
- Braking distance is the distance your vehicle will travel, in ideal conditions; while you are braking. At 55 mph on dry pavement with good brakes, it can take about 216 feet.
- Total stopping distance is the total minimum distance your vehicle has traveled, in ideal conditions; with everything considered, including perception distance, reaction distance and braking distance, until you can bring your vehicle to a complete stop. At 55 mph, your vehicle will travel a minimum of 419 feet.

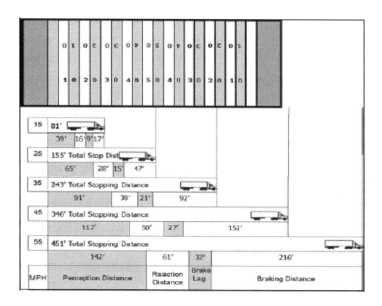

Things to remember:
- When you double your speed, it takes four times as much distance to stop your vehicle.
- Your vehicle will have four times the destructive power in a crash.
- You can't steer or brake a vehicle unless you have traction. Traction is the friction between the tires and the road. Reduce your speed on wet and slippery roads.
- Wet roads can double stopping distance. Reduce your speed by about 1/3 on a wet road. For example slow down from 55 mph to 35 mph.
- On packed snow, reduce your speed by ½ or more.
- If the road is icy, reduce your speed to a crawl. Stop driving as soon as you can.
- Empty trucks require greater stopping distance. An empty vehicle has less traction. The brakes are designed to control the maximum weight of the unit; therefore, the brakes lock up more readily when the trailer is empty or lightly loaded. This can cause skidding and loss of control.

Slippery surfaces

- Shady parts of the road will remain icy and slippery long after open areas have melted.
- When the temperature drops, bridges will freeze before the road will. Be especially careful when the temperature is close to 32 degrees Fahrenheit.
- Slight melting will make ice wet. Wet ice is much more slippery than ice that is not wet.
- Black ice is a thin layer that is clear enough that you can see the road underneath it. It makes the road look wet. Any time the temperature is below freezing and the road looks wet, watch out for black ice.
- An easy way to check for ice is to open the window and feel the front of the mirror, mirror support, or antenna. If there's ice on these, the road surface is probably starting to ice up.
- Right after it starts to rain, the water mixes with oil left on the road by vehicles. This makes the road very slippery. If the rain continues, it will wash the oil away.

Hydroplaning

In some weather, water or slush collects on the road. When this happens, your vehicle can hydroplane. It's like water skiing--the tires lose their contact with the road and have little or no traction. You may not be able to steer or brake. You can regain control by releasing the accelerator and pushing in the clutch. This will slow your vehicle and let the wheels turn freely. If the vehicle is hydroplaning, do not use the brakes to slow down. If the drive wheels start to skid, push in the clutch to let them turn freely. It does not take a lot of water to cause hydroplaning. Hydroplaning can occur at speeds as low as 30 mph if there is a lot of water. Hydroplaning is more likely if tire pressure is low, or the tread is worn. (The grooves in a tire carry away the water; if they aren't deep, they don't work well.) Road surfaces where water can collect can create conditions that cause a vehicle to hydroplane. Watch for clear reflections, tire splashes, and raindrops on the road. These are indications of standing water.

Speed and curves

Drivers must adjust their speed for curves in the road. If you take a curve too fast, two things can happen. The tires can lose their traction and continue straight ahead, so you skid off the road. Or, the tires may keep their traction and the vehicle rolls over. Tests have shown that trucks with a high center of gravity can roll over at the posted speed limit for a curve. It is always best to slow to a safe speed when taking large curves. Don't ever exceed the posted speed limit for the curve. Remember, the posted safe speeds are meant for cars. Slow to a safe speed before you enter a curve. Braking in a curve is dangerous because it is easier to lock the wheels and cause a skid. Be in a gear that will let you accelerate slightly in the curve. This will help you keep control. When you must use low beams, make sure to slow down.

Speed and distance ahead

You should always be able to stop within the distance you can see ahead. Fog, rain, or other conditions may require that you slow down to be able to stop in the distance you can see. At night, you can't see as far with low beams as you can with high beams.

Speed in traffic

When you're driving in heavy traffic, the safest speed is the speed of other vehicles. Vehicles going the same direction at the same speed are not likely to run into one another. In many states, speed limits are lower for trucks and buses than for cars. It can vary as much as 15 mph. Use extra caution when you change lanes or pass on these roadways. Drive at the speed of the traffic, if you can without going at an illegal or unsafe speed. Keep a safe following distance. The main reason drivers exceed speed limits is to save time. But, anyone trying to drive faster than the speed of traffic will not be able to save much time. The risks involved are not worth it. If you go faster than the speed of other traffic, you'll have to keep passing other vehicles. This increases the chance of a crash, and it is more tiring. Fatigue increases the chance of a crash. Going with the flow of traffic is safer and easier.

Speed on downgrades

Your vehicle's speed will increase on downgrades because of gravity. Your most important objective is to select and maintain a speed that is not too fast for the:
- Total weight of the vehicle and cargo.
- Length of the grade.
- Steepness of the grade.
- Road conditions.
- Weather.

If a speed limit is posted, or there is a sign indicating "Maximum Safe Speed," never exceed the speed shown. Also, look for and heed warning signs indicating the length and steepness of the grade. You must use the braking effect of the engine as the principal way of controlling your speed on downgrades. The braking effect of the engine is greatest when it is near the governed rpms and the transmission is in the lower gears. Save your brakes so you will be able to slow or stop as required by road and traffic conditions. Shift your transmission to a low gear before starting down the grade and use the proper braking techniques. Please read carefully the section on going down long, steep downgrades safely in "Mountain Driving."

Work zones

Speeding traffic is the number one cause of injury and death in roadway work zones. Observe the posted speed limits at all times when approaching and driving through a work zone. Watch your speedometer, and don't allow your speed to creep up as you drive through long sections of road construction. Decrease your speed for adverse weather or road conditions. Decrease your speed even further when a worker is close to the roadway. Not only is this saving the lives of the workers, but remember that tickets for speeding in work zones are nearly double that of a normal ticket. It pays to slow down.

Braking

If someone suddenly pulls out in front of you, your natural response is to hit the brakes. This is a good response if there's enough distance to stop, and you use the brakes correctly.

Controlled braking
With this method, you apply the brakes as hard as you can without locking the wheels. Keep steering wheel movements very small while doing this. If you need to make a larger steering adjustment or if the wheels lock, release the brakes. Re-apply the brakes as soon as you can. You never want to lose control while braking. It is important not to panic.

Stab braking
- Apply your brakes all the way.
- Release brakes when wheels lock up.
- Release the brakes when the wheels lock up.
- As soon as the wheels start rolling, apply the brakes fully again. (It can take up to one second for the wheels to start rolling after you release the brakes. If you re-apply the brakes before the wheels start rolling, the vehicle won't straighten out.)

Don't jam on the brakes. Emergency braking does not mean pushing down on the brake pedal as hard as you can. That will only keep the wheels locked up and cause a skid. If the wheels are skidding, you cannot control the vehicle.

Brake failure
Brakes kept in good condition rarely fail. Most hydraulic brake failures occur for one of two reasons:
- Loss of hydraulic pressure.
- Brake fade on long hills.

Loss of hydraulic pressure: When the system won't build up pressure, the brake pedal will feel spongy or go to the floor. Here are some things you can do:
- Downshift. Putting the vehicle into a lower gear will help to slow the vehicle.
- Pump the brakes. Sometimes pumping the brake pedal will generate enough hydraulic pressure to stop the vehicle.
- Use the parking brake. The parking or emergency brake is separate from the hydraulic brake system. Therefore, it can be used to slow the vehicle. However, be sure to press the release button or pull the release lever at the same time you use the emergency brake so you can adjust the brake pressure and keep the wheels from locking up.
- Find an escape route. While slowing the vehicle, look for an escape route--an open field, side street, or escape ramp. Turning uphill is a good way to slow and stop the vehicle. Make sure the vehicle does not start rolling backward after you stop. Put it in low gear, apply the parking brake, and, if necessary, roll back into some obstacle to stop.

Brake failure on downgrades: Going slow enough and braking properly will almost always prevent brake failure on long downgrades. Once the brakes have failed, however, you are going to have to look outside your vehicle for something to stop it. Your best hope is an escape ramp. If there is one available, there will be signs letting you know where each location is. Ramps are usually located a few miles from the top of the downgrade. Every year, hundreds of drivers avoid injury by using escape ramps. Some escape ramps use soft gravel that resists the motion of the vehicle and brings it to a stop. Others turn uphill, using the hill to stop the vehicle and soft gravel to hold it in place. Any driver who loses brakes going downhill should use an escape ramp if it's available. If you don't use it, your chances of having a serious crash may be much greater. If no escape ramp is available, take the least hazardous escape route you can--such as an open field or a side road that flattens out or turns uphill. Make the move as soon as you know your brakes don't work. The longer you wait, the faster the vehicle will go, and the harder it will be to stop.

Tire failure

Quickly recognizing you have a tire failure will let you give you more time to react. Having just a few extra seconds to remember what it is you're supposed to do can help you. The major signs of tire failure are:

- The loud "bang" of a blowout is an easily recognizable sign. It can take a few seconds for your vehicle to react. You might even think it was another vehicle. Any time you hear a tire blow, it would be safest to assume it is yours. Always check.
- Vibration. If the vehicle thumps or vibrates heavily, it may be a sign that one of the tires has gone flat. With a rear tire, that may be the only sign you get.
- Feel. If the steering feels "heavy," it is probably a sign that one of the front tires has failed. Sometimes, failure of a rear tire will cause the vehicle to slide back and forth or "fishtail." However, dual rear tires usually prevent this.

Respond to tire failure. When a tire fails, your vehicle is in danger. You must immediately:

- Hold the steering wheel firmly. If a front tire fails, it can twist the steering wheel out of your hand. The only way to prevent this is to keep a firm grip on the steering wheel with both hands at all times.
- Stay off the brake. It's natural to want to brake in an emergency. However, braking when a tire has failed could cause loss of control. Unless you're about to run into something, stay off the brake until the vehicle has slowed down. Then brake very gently, pull off the road, and stop.
- Check the tires. After you've come to a stop, get out and check all the tires. Do this even if the vehicle seems to be handling all right. If one of your dual tires goes, the only way you may know it is by getting out and looking at it.

Steering to avoid crashing

- Stopping is not always the safest thing to do in an emergency. When you don't have enough room to stop, you may have to steer away from what's ahead. Remember, you can almost always turn to miss an obstacle more quickly than you can stop. (However, top-heavy vehicles and tractors with multiple trailers may flip over.)
- Keep both hands on the steering wheel. In order to turn quickly, you must have a firm grip on the steering wheel with both hands. The best way to have both hands on the wheel, if there is an emergency, is to keep them there all the time.
- Do not apply the brakes while you are turning. This could cause your wheels to lock and you could skid out of control.
- Do not turn any more than needed to clear whatever is in your way. The more sharply you turn, the greater the chances of a skid or rollover.
- Be prepared to "countersteer," that is, to turn the wheel back in the other direction, once you've passed whatever was in your path. Unless you are prepared to countersteer, you won't be able to do it quickly enough. You should think of emergency steering and countersteering as two parts of one driving action.
- If an oncoming driver has drifted into your lane, a move to your right is best. If that driver realizes what has happened, the natural response will be to return to his or her own lane.
- If something is blocking your path, the best direction to steer will depend on the situation. You must be prepared for anything.

In some emergencies, you may have to drive off the road. It may be less risky than facing a collision with another vehicle. Most shoulders are strong enough to support the weight of a large vehicle and, therefore, offer an available escape route. Here are some guidelines, if you do leave the road.

- Avoid braking. If possible, avoid using the brakes until your speed has dropped to about 20 mph. Then brake very gently to avoid skidding on a loose surface.
- Keep one set of wheels on the pavement, if possible. This helps to maintain control.
- Stay on the shoulder. If the shoulder is clear, stay on it until your vehicle has come to a stop. Signal and check your mirrors before pulling back onto the road.

Returning to the road

If you are forced to return to the road before you can stop, use the following procedure:

- Hold the wheel tightly and turn sharply enough to get right back on the road safely.
- Don't try to edge gradually back on the road. If you do, your tires might grab unexpectedly and you could lose control.
- When both front tires are on the paved surface, countersteer immediately. The two turns should be made as a single "steer-countersteer" move.

Skid control and recovery

A skid happens whenever the tires lose their grip on the road. This is caused in one of four ways:

- Over-braking. Braking too hard and locking up the wheels. Skids also can occur when using the speed retarder when the road is slippery.
- Over-steering. Turning the wheels more sharply than the vehicle can turn.
- Over-acceleration. Supplying too much power to the drive wheels, causing them to spin.
- Driving too fast. Most serious skids result from driving too fast for road conditions. Drivers who adjust their driving to conditions don't over-accelerate and don't have to over-brake or over-steer from too much speed.

Drive-wheel skids

By far the most common skid is one in which the rear wheels lose traction through excessive braking or acceleration. Skids caused by acceleration usually happen on ice or snow. Taking your foot off the accelerator can easily stop them. (If it is very slippery, push the clutch in. Otherwise, the engine can keep the wheels from rolling freely and regaining traction.) Rear wheel braking skids occur when the rear drive wheels lock. Because locked wheels have less traction than rolling wheels, the rear wheels usually slide sideways in an attempt to "catch up" with the front wheels. In a bus or straight truck, the vehicle will slide sideways in a "spin out." With vehicles towing trailers, a drive-wheel skid can let the trailer push the towing vehicle sideways, causing a sudden jackknife.

Hazardous Conditions

Driving becomes hazardous when visibility is reduced, or when the road surface is covered with rain, snow or ice. Slow down and increase your following distance.

Night driving

You are at greater risk when you drive at night. Drivers can't see hazards as quickly as in daylight, so they have less time to respond. Drivers caught by surprise are less able to avoid a crash. The problems of night driving involve the driver, the roadway, and the vehicle.

Driver

People can't see as sharply at night or in dim light. Also, their eyes need time to adjust to seeing in dim light. Most people have noticed this when walking into a dark movie theater.

- Drivers can be blinded for a short time by bright light. It takes time to recover from this blindness. Older drivers are especially bothered by glare. Most people have been temporarily blinded by camera flash units or by the high beams of an oncoming vehicle. It can take several seconds to recover from glare. Even two seconds of glare blindness can be dangerous. A vehicle going 55 mph will travel more than half the distance of a football field during that time. Don't look directly at bright lights when driving. Look at the right side of the road. Watch the sidelines when someone coming toward you has very bright lights on.
- Fatigue (being tired) and lack of alertness are bigger problems at night. The body's need for sleep is beyond a person's control. Most people are less alert at night, especially after midnight. This is particularly true if you have been driving for a long time. Drivers may not see hazards as soon, or react as quickly, so the chance of a crash is greater.
- If you are sleepy, the only safe cure is to get off the road and get some sleep. If you don't, you risk your life and the lives of others.

Roadway

- Poor lighting. In the daytime there is usually enough light to see well. This is not true at night. Some areas may have bright street lights, but many areas will have poor lighting. On most roads you will probably have to depend entirely on your headlights. Less light means you will not be able to see hazards as well as in daytime. Road users who do not have lights are hard to see. There are many accidents at night involving pedestrians, joggers, bicyclists, and animals.
- Even when there are lights, the road scene can be confusing. Traffic signals and hazards can be hard to see against a background of signs, shop windows, and other lights. Drive slower when lighting is poor or confusing. Drive slowly enough to be sure you can stop in the distance you can see ahead.
- Drunk drivers. Drunk drivers and drivers under the influence of drugs are a hazard to themselves and to you. Be especially alert around the closing times for bars and taverns. Watch for drivers who have trouble staying in their lane or maintaining speed, who stop without reason, or show other signs of being under the influence of alcohol or drugs.

Vehicle

At night, you must depend a lot on your headlights functioning to see and be seen by other motorists. Your sight is still limited at night, even with the help of your headlights. You need to make necessary adjustments for these limitations.

- Make sure you aren't going faster than it would take to stop within the distance that you can see ahead of you. With your low beams, you can see ahead about 250 feet. With your high beams, you can see ahead between 300 and 500 feet. These are approximations of course. It will vary with each driver. You should make sure you can stop between the approximate distances by adjusting your speed accordingly. This will also vary by the size of the load you are carrying and road conditions. Take everything into account when driving at night.
- Make sure that your headlights are clean and adjusted properly. Dirty headlights do not provide the same amount of light that clean ones do. Dirty headlights defeat their purpose. It makes it much harder for you to see and for others to see you. Proper headlight maintenance is very important.
- Be sure that all lights and reflectors are clean and working so that other drivers can see you. A thorough truck wash should keep you good to go for a while. You just have to continue to monitor everything to stay safe. Clean windows and lights are very important when it comes to driving in any condition. The lights you want to check include:
  - Headlights (high and low beams)
  - Tail lights
  - Turn signals
  - Brake lights
  - Marker lights
  - Clearance lights
  - Identification lights

You should be able to stop within the distance that you can see ahead.

With low beams you can see 250 feet ahead

With high beams you can see 300 to 500 feet ahead

Fog

Fog reflects light and can reflect your own headlights back into your eyes. Use only your low beams. Look for road edge markings to guide you. Even light fog reduces your ability to see and judge distances. If possible, pull off the road and wait until the fog has lifted. If you must drive, be sure to:
- Obey all fog-related warning signs.
- Reduce you speed.
- Turn on all your lights.
- Use only your low beams.
- Be prepared for sudden stops.

Cold weather driving

Vehicle checks

While performing your pre-trip inspection, you will want to pay close attention to a list of things. First, be sure that the following systems are working properly and that you are confident you know how to use them before operating the vehicle.
- Defrosting and heating equipment: Make sure the defrosters work. They are needed for safe driving. Make sure the heater is working, and that you know how to operate it. If you use other heaters and expect to need them (e.g., mirror heaters, battery box heaters, fuel tank heaters), check their operation.
- Lights and reflectors: Make sure the lights and reflectors are clean. Lights and reflectors are especially important during bad weather. Check from time to time during bad weather to make sure they are clean and working properly.
- Windows and mirrors: Remove any ice, snow, etc., from the windshield, windows, and mirrors before starting. Use a windshield scraper, snow brush, and windshield defroster as necessary. Hand Holds, Steps, and Deck Plates. Remove all ice and snow from hand holds, steps, and deck plates. This will reduce the danger of slipping.
- Radiator shutters and winterfront: Remove ice from the radiator shutters. Make sure the winterfront is not closed too tightly. If the shutters freeze shut or the winterfront is closed too much, the engine may overheat and stop.
- Exhaust system: Exhaust system leaks are especially dangerous when cab ventilation may be poor (windows rolled up, etc.). Loose connections could permit poisonous carbon monoxide to leak into your vehicle. Carbon monoxide gas will cause you to be sleepy. In large enough amounts it can kill you. Check the exhaust system for loose parts and for sounds and signs of leaks.
- Coolant level and antifreeze amount: Make sure the cooling system is full and there is enough antifreeze in the system to protect against freezing. This can be checked with a special coolant tester.
- Wipers and washers: Make sure the windshield wiper blades are in good condition. Make sure the wiper blades press against the window hard enough to wipe the windshield clean, otherwise they may not sweep off snow properly. Make sure the windshield washer works and there is washing fluid in the washer reservoir.
- Tires: Make sure you have enough tread on your tires. The drive tires must provide traction to push the rig over wet pavement and through snow. The steering tires must have traction to steer the vehicle. Enough tread is especially important in winter conditions. You must have at least 4/32 inch tread depth in every major groove on front tires and at least 2/32 inch on other tires. More would be better. Use a gauge to determine if you have enough tread for safe driving.
- Tire chains: You may find yourself in conditions where you can't drive without chains, even to get to a place of safety. Carry the right number of chains and extra cross-links. Make sure they will fit your drive tires. Check the chains for broken hooks, worn or broken cross-links, and bent or broken side chains. Learn how to put the chains on before you need to do it in snow and ice.

Driving tips

- Drive slowly and smoothly on slippery roads. If it is very slippery, you shouldn't drive at all. Stop at the first safe place.
- Adjust turning and braking to conditions. Make turns as gently as possible. Do not brake any harder than necessary, and don't use the engine brake or speed retarder. (They can cause the driving wheels to skid on slippery surfaces.)
- Adjust speed to conditions. Don't pass slower vehicles unless necessary. Go slowly and watch far enough ahead to keep a steady speed. Avoid having to slow down and speed up. Take curves at slower speeds and don't brake while in curves. Be aware that as the temperature rises to the point where ice begins to melt, the road becomes even more slippery. Slow down more.
- Adjust space to conditions. Don't drive alongside other vehicles. Keep a longer following distance. When you see a traffic jam ahead, slow down or stop to wait for it to clear. Try hard to anticipate stops early and slow down gradually. Watch for snowplows, as well as salt and sand trucks, and give them plenty of room.

Wet brakes

When driving in heavy rain or deep standing water, your brakes will get wet. Water in the brakes can cause the brakes to be weak, to apply unevenly, or to grab. This can cause lack of braking power, wheel lockups, pulling to one side or the other, and jackknife if you pull a trailer. Avoid driving through deep puddles or flowing water if possible. If not, you should:

- Slow down and place transmission in a low gear.
- Gently put on the brakes. This presses linings against brake drums or discs and keeps mud, silt, sand, and water from getting in.
- Increase engine rpm and cross the water while keeping light pressure on the brakes.
- When out of the water, maintain light pressure on the brakes for a short distance to heat them up and dry them out.
- Make a test stop when safe to do so. Check behind to make sure no one is following, then apply the brakes to be sure they work well. If not, dry them out further as described above. (CAUTION: Do not apply too much brake pressure and accelerator at the same time, or you can overheat brake drums and linings.)

Hot weather driving

<u>Vehicle checks</u>
Do a normal pre-trip inspection, but pay special attention to the following items.

- Tires: Check the tire mounting and air pressure. Inspect the tires every two hours or every 100 miles when driving in very hot weather. Air pressure increases with temperature. Do not let air out or the pressure will be too low when the tires cool off. If a tire is too hot to touch, remain stopped until the tire cools off. Otherwise the tire may blow out or catch fire.
- Engine oil: The engine oil helps keep the engine cool, as well as lubricating it. Make sure there is enough engine oil. If you have an oil temperature gauge, make sure the temperature is within the proper range while you are driving.
- Engine coolant: Before starting out, make sure the engine cooling system has enough water and antifreeze according to the engine manufacturer's directions. (Antifreeze helps the engine under hot conditions as well as cold conditions.) When driving, check the water temperature or coolant temperature gauge from time to time. Make sure that it remains in the normal range. If the gauge goes above the highest safe temperature, there may be something wrong that could lead to engine failure and possibly fire. Stop driving as soon as safely possible and try to find out what is wrong. Some vehicles have sight glasses, see-through coolant overflow containers, or coolant recovery containers. These permit you to check the coolant level while the engine is hot. If the container is not part of the pressurized system, the cap can be safely removed and coolant added even when the engine is at operating temperature. Never remove the radiator cap or any part of the pressurized system until the system has cooled. Steam and boiling water can spray under pressure and cause severe burns. If you can touch the radiator cap with your bare hand, it is probably cool enough to open. If coolant has to be added to a system without a recovery tank or overflow tank, follow these steps:
    - Shut engine off.
    - Wait until engine has cooled.
    - Protect hands (use gloves or a thick cloth).
    - Turn radiator cap slowly to the first stop, which releases the pressure seal. • Step back while pressure is released from cooling system.
    - When all pressure has been released, press down on the cap and turn it further to remove it.
    - Visually check level of coolant and add more coolant if necessary.
    - Replace cap and turn all the way to the closed position.
- Engine belts: Learn how to check v-belt tightness on your vehicle by pressing on the belts. Loose belts will not turn the water pump and/or fan properly. This will result in overheating. Also, check belts for cracking or other signs of wear.
- Hoses: Make sure coolant hoses are in good condition. A broken hose while driving can lead to engine failure and even fire.

<u>Driving tips</u>
Watch for bleeding tar. Tar in the road pavement frequently rises to the surface in very hot weather. Spots where tar "bleeds" to the surface are very slippery. Go slowly enough to prevent overheating. High speeds create more heat for tires and the engine. In desert conditions the heat may build up to the point where it is dangerous. The heat will increase chances of tire failure or even fire, and engine failure.

Mountain driving

In mountain driving, gravity plays a major role. On any upgrade, gravity slows you down. The steeper the grade, the longer the grade, and/or the heavier the load--the more you will have to use lower gears to climb hills or mountains. In coming down long, steep downgrades, gravity causes the speed of your vehicle to increase. You must select an appropriate safe speed, then use a low gear, and proper braking techniques. You should plan ahead and obtain information about any long, steep grades along your planned route of travel. If possible, talk to other drivers who are familiar with the grades to find out what speeds are safe.   You must go slowly enough so your brakes can hold you back without getting too hot. If the brakes become too hot, they may start to "fade." This means you have to apply them harder and harder to get the same stopping power. If you continue to use the brakes hard, they can keep fading until you cannot slow down or stop at all.

Safe speed

Your most important consideration is to select a speed that is not too fast for the:
- Total weight of the vehicle and cargo.
- Length of the grade.
- Steepness of the grade.
- Road conditions.
- Weather
- If a speed limit is posted, or there is a sign indicating "Maximum Safe Speed," never exceed the speed shown. Also, look for and heed warning signs indicating the length and steepness of the grade.
- You must use the braking effect of the engine as the principal way of controlling your speed. The braking effect of the engine is greatest when it is near the governed RPMs and the transmission is in the lower gears.
- Save your brakes so you will be able to slow or stop as required by road and traffic conditions.
- Shift the transmission to a low gear before starting down the grade. Do not try to downshift after your speed has already built up. You will not be able to shift into a lower gear. You may not even be able to get back into any gear and all engine braking effect will be lost. Forcing an automatic transmission into a lower gear at high speed could damage the transmission and also lead to loss of all engine braking effect.
- Use the proper braking technique. Use your brakes on a long, steep downgrade plus the braking power of your engine. When your vehicle is in the proper low gear, use this braking technique:
- Know where the escape ramps are located on your route. Escape ramps have been built on many steep downgrades. They are made to stop runaway vehicles without injuring drivers and passengers. Escape ramps use a long bed of loose soft material to slow runaway vehicles. Use them if you lose your brakes.

43

Railroad crossing

At many highway-rail grade crossings, the crossbuck sign has flashing red lights and bells. When the lights begin to flash, stop! A train is approaching. You are required to yield the right- of-way to the train. If there is more than one track, make sure all tracks are clear before crossing. Many railroad-highway crossings also have gates with flashing red lights and bells. Stop when the lights begin to flash and before the gate lowers across the road lane. Remain stopped until the gates go up and the lights have stopped flashing. Proceed when it is safe. Never attempt to race a train to a crossing. It is extremely difficult to judge the speed of an approaching train.

- Speed must be reduced in accordance with your ability to see approaching trains in any direction, and speed must be held to a point which will permit you to stop short of the tracks in case a stop is necessary.
- Because of noise inside your vehicle, you cannot expect to hear the train horn until the train is dangerously close to the crossing.
- You should not rely solely upon the presence of warning signals, gates, or flagmen to warn of the approach of trains.
- Double tracks require a double check.
- Remember that a train on one track may hide a train on the other track. Look both ways before crossing. After one train has cleared a crossing, be sure no other trains are near before starting across the tracks.
- Vehicles that have low ground clearance, such as drop frame trailers and car carriers can cause your vehicle to hang up on railroad crossings with steep approaches. If you get hung up on a railroad crossing, call 9-1-1 immediately so that the scheduled trains can be notified to stop.
- Be sure you can get all the way across the tracks before you begin to cross.
- Do not shift gears when crossing railroad tracks.
- A full stop is required at grade crossings whenever:
  - The nature of the cargo makes a stop mandatory under state or federal regulations.
  - Such a stop is otherwise required by law.
- When stopping be sure to:
  - Check for traffic behind you while stopping gradually. Use a pullout lane, if available.
  - Turn on your four-way emergency flashers.

Equipment failures

Brake failures
Brakes kept in good condition rarely fail. Most hydraulic brake failures occur for one of two reasons:
- Loss of hydraulic pressure
- Brake fade on long hills

When the system won't build up pressure, the brake pedal will feel spongy or go to the floor. Here are some things you can do:
- Downshift. Putting the vehicle into a lower gear will help to slow the vehicle.
- Pump the brakes. Sometimes pumping the brake pedal will generate enough hydraulic pressure to stop the vehicle.

Airbrake fading or failure
Excessive use of the service brakes results in overheating and leads to brake fade. Brake fade results from excessive heat causing chemical changes in the brake lining, which reduce friction, and also causing expansion of the brake drums. As the overheated drums expand, the brake shoes and linings have to move farther to contact the drums, and the force of this contact is reduced. Continued overuse may increase brake fade until the vehicle cannot be slowed down or stopped. Brake fade is also affected by adjustment. To safely control a vehicle, every brake must do its share of the work. Brakes out of adjustment will stop doing their share before those that are

in adjustment. The other brakes can then overheat and fade, and there will not be enough braking available to control the vehicle(s). Brakes can get out of adjustment quickly, especially when they are hot. Therefore, check brake adjustment often

Tire failure
The sooner that you realize that a tire has failed, the more time you will have to react to the situation. The recognizable signs of tire failure are:
- Sound. You may hear a loud bang that often accompanies a blowout. However, you may mistake the noise for another vehicle as yours will not have an immediate effect on your driving. It is best to always assume it was one of yours and to use your mirrors to check.
- Vibration. If your vehicle vibrates, you may have a tire failure. With a rear tire, this may be the only sign you get as tandem wheels often compensate for the failed tire.
- Feel. If it becomes harder than usual to control your steering, one of the front tires has probably failed.

If a tire fails, take the following steps:
- Maintain a solid grip on the steering wheel. If a front tire fails, it can cause the wheel to twist out of your hands. Keep both hands on the wheel at all times.
- Stay off the brakes. If you brake during a tire failure, it could cause you to lose control of the vehicle. Unless it is necessary for the safety of you or fellow drivers, stay off the brake until the vehicle has slowed down on its own (engine brakes can help this). Then, brake gently and pull off the road.
- Check the tires even if the vehicle seems to be handling normally. Many times you won't know that a dual tire is flat unless you look at it.

Crashes

As a professional driver, if you are in a crash and not seriously hurt; you need to take three steps to prevent further damage or injury to yourself or others:
- Protect the scene (keep people away):
  o Protect the area to prevent another crash. This is the first thing you need to do.
  o If your vehicle is involved in the crash, try to move it out of the roadway. This will help prevent additional crashes.
  o If you are stopping to help at the scene of a crash, park far away from the crash. The area around the crash will be needed by emergency vehicles.
  o Put on your flashers.
  o Set out reflective triangles to warn other traffic. Make sure that other drivers will see them in time to avoid another crash by following the same distance rules as if you were stalled on the side of the road.
- Notify the authorities as soon as possible (inform them of your cargo if hazardous). If you have a CB radio or cell phone, put out a call over the emergency channel or dial 911 before leaving your vehicle. If you have no way to contact authorities, wait until the crash scene has been protected, then call or send someone to call the police. Remember to determine where you are before contacting anyone so you can provide an accurate location of the crash.
- Care for the injured (never move them unless they are able to move themselves). If a qualified person is helping the injured, stay out of their way unless you are asked to assist. Otherwise, make every effort to help anyone who could be injured. Don't move a severely injured person unless there is a danger of fire or passing traffic makes it necessary. Stop heavy bleeding by applying direct pressure to the wound. Keep the injured person warm.

Fires

You might have to control minor truck fires on the road. However, unless you have the training and equipment to do so safely, don't fight hazardous materials fires. Dealing with hazardous materials fires requires special training and protective gear. When you discover a fire, call for help. You may use the fire extinguisher to keep minor truck fires from spreading to cargo before firefighters arrive. Feel trailer doors to see if they are hot before opening them. If hot, you may have a cargo fire and should not open the doors. Opening doors lets air in and may make the fire flare up. Without air, many fires only smolder until firemen arrive, doing less damage. If your cargo is already on fire, it is not safe to fight the fire. Keep the shipping papers with you to give to emergency personnel as soon as they arrive. Warn other people of the danger and keep them away. If you discover a cargo leak, identify the hazardous materials leaking by using shipping papers, labels, or package location.

Do not touch any leaking material--many people injure themselves by touching hazardous materials. Do not try to identify the material or find the source of a leak by smell. Toxic gases can destroy your sense of smell and can injure or kill you even if they don't smell. Never eat, drink, or smoke around a leak or spill. If hazardous materials are spilling from your vehicle, do not move it any more than safety requires. You may move off the road and away from places where people gather, if doing so serves safety. Only move your vehicle if you can do so without danger to yourself or others.

Hazardous materials

Rules for all commercial drivers
Hazardous materials are products that pose a risk to health, safety, and property during transportation. The term often is shortened to HAZMAT, which you may see on road signs, or to HM in government regulations. Hazardous materials include explosives, various types of gas, solids, flammable and combustible liquid, and other materials. Because of the risks involved and the potential consequences these risks impose, all levels of government regulate the handling of hazardous materials. The Hazardous Materials Regulations (HMR) is found in parts 100 - 185 of title 49 of the Code of Federal Regulations. The common reference for these regulations is 49 CFR 100 – 185. The table below lists 9 hazard classes:

Class	Division	Name of Class or Division	Example
1	1.1	Explosives (Mass Detonations)	Dynamite
	1.2	Projection Hazards	Ammunition for Cannons
	1.3	Mass Fire Hazards	Display Fireworks
	1.4	Minor Hazards	Small Arms Ammunition
	1.5	Very Insensitive	Blasting Agents
	1.6	Extremely Insensitive	Explosive Devices
2	2.1	Flammable Gases	Propane
	2.2	Non-Flammable Gases	Helium
	2.3	Poisonous/Toxic Gases	Fluorine, Compressed
3	---	Flammable Liquids	Gasoline, Diesel Fuel
4	4.1	Flammable Solids	Ammonium Picrate, Wetted White
	4.2	Spontaneous Combustible	Phosphorus
	4.3	Dangerous When Wet	Sodium
5	5.1	Oxidizers	Ammonium Nitrate
	5.2	Organic Peroxides	Methyl Ethyl Ketone Peroxide
6	6.1	Poison (Toxic Material)	Potassium Cyanide
	6.2	Infectious Substances	Anthrax Virus
7	---	Radioactive	Uranium
8	---	Corrosives	Battery Fluid
9	---	Miscellaneous Hazardous Materials	Polychlorinated Biphenyls (PCB)
None	---	ORM-D (Other Regulated Material-Domestic)	Food Flavorings, Medicines, Cleaning Compounds, and Other Consumer Commodities
None	---	Combustible Liquids	Fuel Oil

You must follow the rules for transporting hazardous materials. These rules ensure safe drivers and equipment. They also tell you how to contain the product and how to communicate its risk. The regulations require vehicles transporting certain types or quantities of hazardous materials to display diamond-shaped, square on point, warning signs called placards. You must have a commercial driver license (CDL) with a hazardous materials endorsement before you drive any size vehicle that is used to transport hazardous material as defined in 49 CFR 383.5. You must pass a written test about the regulations and requirements to get this endorsement.

Containment rules
Transporting hazardous materials can be risky. The regulations are intended to protect you, those around you, and the environment. They tell shippers how to package the materials safely and drivers how to load, transport, and unload the material. These are called "containment rules."

Communicating the risk

To communicate the risk, shippers must warn drivers and others about the material's hazards. The regulations require shippers to put hazard warning labels on packages, provide proper shipping papers, emergency response information, and placards. These steps communicate the hazard to the shipper, the carrier, and the driver. Placards are 10 ¾ inches on each side and are diamond-shaped. Cargo tanks and other bulk packaging display the I.D. number of their contents on placards or orange panels. A placarded vehicle must have at least 4 identical placards. They are placed on the front, rear and both sides of the vehicle. Not all vehicles that carry hazardous materials need placards. The regulations about placards are given in Section 9 of this driver's manual. You can drive a vehicle carrying hazardous materials if it does not require placards. If it requires placards, you may not drive it unless you have a hazardous material endorsement on your commercial driver's license.

Roles in hazardous material transportation

Shipper:

- Sends products from one place to another by truck, rail, vessel, or airplane.
- Uses the hazardous materials regulations to determine the product's:
  - Proper shipping name.
  - Hazard class.
  - Identification number.
  - Packing group.
  - Correct packaging.
  - Correct label and markings.
  - Correct placards.
- Must package, mark, and label the materials; prepare shipping papers; provide emergency response information; and supply placards.
- Certify on the shipping paper that the shipment has been prepared according to the rules (unless you are pulling cargo tanks supplied by you or your employer).

Carrier:

- Takes the shipment from the shipper to its destination.
- Prior to transportation, checks that the shipper correctly described, marked, labeled, and otherwise prepared the shipment for transportation.
- Refuses improper shipments.
- Reports accidents and incidents involving hazardous materials to the proper government agency.

Driver:

- Makes sure the shipper has identified, marked, and labeled the hazardous materials properly.
- Refuses leaking packages and shipments.
- Placards vehicle when loading, if required.
- Safely transports the shipment without delay.
- Follows all special rules about transporting hazardous materials.
- Keeps hazardous material shipping papers and emergency response information in the proper place.

General Knowledge Test

1. What is the minimum amount of tread depth that your tires should have?
    a. There should be at least four-thirty seconds tread depth in every major groove on the front wheels and at least two-thirty seconds inch tread on all other wheels.
    b. There should be at least one-inch tread depth in every major groove on all wheels.
    c. There should be at least four-thirty seconds inch tread depth in every major groove on all wheels.

2. How do you test hydraulic brakes for a leak?
    a. With the vehicle under way at a low speed, apply firm pressure, stopping the vehicle as quickly as possible.
    b. With the vehicle stopped, push down the brake pedal and do not release for at least five seconds.
    c. With the vehicle stopped, pump the brake pedal three times. Apply firm pressure, and then hold for five seconds.

3. How do you test hydraulic brakes for their stopping action?
    a. Go about five miles per hour. Push the brake pedal firmly.
    b. With the vehicle stopped, pump the brake pedal three times. Apply firm pressure, and then hold for five seconds.
    c. With the vehicle stopped, push the brake pedal firmly, and then hold for five seconds.

4. How does tire pressure affect hydroplaning?
    a. Hydroplaning is not affected by tire pressure.
    b. Hydroplaning is more likely to occur when tire pressure is low.
    c. Hydroplaning is more likely to occur when tires are over inflated.

5. What is the best way to use the brake pedal on a steep downhill grade?
    a. Use a heavy pressure repeatedly.
    b. Avoid using the brakes.
    c. Shift to a lower gear before starting downgrade and use a light, steady pressure on the brake pedal.

6. What is a good rule as to the speed you should go when driving at night?
    a. You should keep your speed slow enough to stop within the range of your headlights.
    b. You do not have to be able to stop within the distance that you can see.
    c. You should never drive so fast as to require your high beams.

7. How many times more distance does it take to stop whenever you double your speed?
    a. Twice as much distance.
    b. Three times as much distance.
    c. Four times as much distance.

8. In checking tires what are some problems that you should look for?
    a. Too much or too little specification information on the sidewalls.
    b. Bad wear, cuts or other damage, tread separation, cut or cracked valve stems. Dual tires that come in contact, mismatched sizes, radial and bias-ply tires used together.
    c. Regrooved, recapped, or retreaded tires on the drive wheels.

9. What are some steering system defects to look for?
    a. Missing nuts, bolts, cotter keys or other parts; bent, loose or broken parts.
    b. Steering wheel play of two degrees.
    c. Steering wheel play of five degrees.

10. What are some defects to look for in the suspension system?
    a. Spring hangers that allow movement of the axle from the proper position; cracked or broken spring hangers; spring hangers or other axle positioning parts that are cracked damaged, or missing.
    b. Oil leaks in the frame or fifth wheel assembly.
    c. Oil leaks in the brake drums.

11. In holding a steering wheel what is the proper way to place your hands?
    a. Loosely with at least one hand on the wheel.
    b. One hand at the top of the wheel and one hand at the bottom of the wheel. In terms of the clock your hands should be at six o'clock and twelve o'clock.
    c. Firmly with both hands and your hands should be on opposite sides of the wheel. In terms of the clock, your hands should be at three o'clock and nine o'clock.

12. What are some things to do when you are backing your vehicle?
    a. First, look at your path. Second, back slowly. Third, back, straight back.
    b. Insist on having a helper to guide you.
    c. Back and turn from the right whenever possible.

13. What is meant by double clutching?
    a. Pushing down on the clutch pedal four times each time you shift gears.
    b. Shifting without using the clutch.
    c. Release the accelerator, push down on the clutch pedal and shift to neutral; then release the clutch pedal; then let the engine and gears slow down to the RPMs required for the nest gear; then push in the clutch pedal and shift to the higher gear.

14. What are two factors in knowing when to shift?
    a. Using transmission speed and clutch stroke.
    b. Using engine speed and road speed.
    c. Using road speed and "feel" of the road.

15. What is one way of knowing when you have the right engine speed and road speed to shift gears?
    a. When the engine is lugging.
    b. By shifting whenever you notice heavy smoke coming from the exhaust stack.
    c. Using the sound of the engine to know when to shift.

16. What is true about downshifting before you reach a long downhill grade?
    a. It helps prevent the brakes from overheating and losing their braking power.
    b. It puts an extra burden on the brake system.
    c. Starting on a downhill grade in low gear increases the chance of the truck picking up speed and going out of control.

17. When should you downshift for a curve?
    a. Slow down to a safe speed and downshift to the proper gear before entering the curve.
    b. Slow down to a safe speed and downshift to the proper gear upon entering the curve.
    c. Slow down to a safe speed and downshift after entering the curve.

18. What is the purpose of brake retarders?
    a. To help slow down the vehicle and to reduce brake wear.
    b. To provide more traction on a slippery surface and enable a vehicle to go faster.
    c. To reduce brake wear and to reduce noise.

19. Should you turn the retarder off when the road is wet, icy, or snow covered?
   a. No, because you need more braking power then.
   b. No, because the engine retarder will have no effect on traction.
   c. Yes, whenever your drive wheels have poor traction the retarder may cause a skid.

20. How far ahead should you look while driving?
   a. 100 feet
   b. Four seconds
   c. 12 to 15 seconds

21. What is a good reason for knowing what the traffic is doing on all sides of you?
   a. Stopping or changing lanes can take time and distance and you need to have room to make these moves safely.
   b. It is always necessary to know when you can make a U-turn.
   c. You need to eliminate all blind spots around you.

22. Should you always be looking into the distance ahead?
   a. Yes, You should be prepared for all problems ahead.
   b. No, you should shift your attention back and forth, near and far.
   c. Yes, by concentrating on the vehicle directly ahead you will be prepared for all emergencies.

23. What is a problem that you can have when using your mirrors?
   a. They never remain in the positions you have placed them.
   b. They are of no help when you are changing lanes.
   c. There are blind spots that your mirrors cannot show you.

24. Where do you place the three reflector triangles if you have to park on the side of a level, straight two-lane road?
   a. Place one within 10 feet of the rear of the vehicle, one about 100 feet to the rear and one about 100 feet from the front of the vehicle.
   b. Place one within 100 feet of the front of the vehicle, one 500 feet from the front of the vehicle and one about 100 feet from the rear of the vehicle.
   c. Place one within 10 feet of the front of the vehicle, one about 100 feet to the front and one about 500 feet to the rear of the vehicle.

25. Where do you place the three reflector triangles if you have to park on the side of a level highway with one-way traffic such as a divided highway?
   a. Place them to the rear of the vehicle; one within 10 feet, one within 100 feet and the other one 200 feet.
   b. Place all of them in front of the vehicle up to 500 feet.
   c. Place two in front of the vehicle at 10 feet and at 100 feet and place one to the rear of the vehicle.

26. What are three factors that add up to total stopping distance with hydraulic-brakes?
   a. Brake lag distance, pedal engaging distance, rolling distance.
   b. Reaction distance, application distance, braking distance.
   c. Perception distance, reaction distance, braking distance.

27. Why do empty trucks usually require greater stopping distance than loaded trucks?
   a. An empty truck has less traction.
   b. An empty truck has more forward momentum.
   c. An empty truck has less brakes.

28. What should you do if your vehicle hydroplanes?
   a. Let up on the clutch.
   b. Release the accelerator and push in the clutch.
   c. Push down on the accelerator releasing the clutch.

29. How long does it take for the average driver to bring a heavy vehicle to a stop when driving 55 miles per hour on dry pavement?
   a. About 100 feet... about 2 seconds
   b. About 200 feet... about 4 seconds.
   c. About 300 feet... about 6 seconds.

30. You are driving a vehicle with a light load. Traffic is moving at 35 miles per hour in a 55 mile per hour zone. What is most likely the safest speed for your vehicle in this situation?
   a. 55 miles per hour
   b. 35 miles per hour
   c. 45 miles per hour

31. When driving how much space should you try to keep in front of you?
   a. One second for each 15 feet of your vehicle length at speeds below 40 miles per hour.
   b. Over 40 miles per hour at least one second for each 10 feet of your vehicle length plus one extra second.
   c. With a forty-foot vehicle leave 5 seconds between you and the vehicle ahead when going below 40 miles per hour.

32. What are some things to do if you are being tailgated?
   a. Avoid quick changes of speed or direction.
   b. Try to reduce your following distance.
   c. Speed up, and flash your taillights on and off.

33. What is one reason that you can never assure that you're safe by reading the heights posted at bridges and overpasses?
   a. Repaving or packed snow may have increased the clearances since the heights were posted.
   b. The weight of a cargo van can change its height with an empty van being lighter or lower.
   c. Some roads can cause your vehicle to tilt.

34. You wish to turn right from a two-lane, two-way street to another. Your vehicle is so long that you must swing wide to make the turn. How should the turn be made?
   a. Start turning wide before you enter the turn.
   b. You may allow your rear trailer wheels to climb over the curb.
   c. Turn wide as you complete the turn.

35. With a large vehicle, if you are turning left, which lane should you use if there are two left turn lanes?
   a. Use either lane.
   b. Use the right hand lane.
   c. Use the left hand lane

36. Since it is difficult to look directly at bright lights when driving, where can you look to avoid the glare of oncoming traffic?
   a. Close your eyes momentarily.
   b. Try to look at the centerline of the highway, watching for the dotted line.
   c. Try to look at the right side of the road, watching the sidelines.

37. What are some items that you <u>must</u> check especially before driving in winter weather?
   a. CB Radio Antenna
   b. Coolant level, windshield washer antifreeze.
   c. AM-FM Radio

38. How often should you check your tires when driving in very hot weather?
   a. Every 2 hours or every 100 miles.
   b. Every time you stop.
   c. Once each hour.

39. Will "fanning" your brakes, allow them to cool so that they won't overheat on a steep downgrade?
   a. Yes, short heavy application of the brakes will prevent the brakes from overheating.
   b. No, the brake system is not affected by "fanning."
   c. No, brake drums cool very slowly and the brakes may begin to fade and have less stopping power when the pressure is not applied steadily.

40. What are some hazards that are frequently seen on the highway?
   a. Workers, children, inattentive drivers, hurrying drivers, impaired drivers, suicides.
   b. Work zones, accidents.
   c. Road edge drop-offs, crashed airplanes, disabled vehicles.

41. What can you do to lessen the chances of having to make a sudden move to avoid hazards?
   a. Keep your vehicle centered in your lane by watching the white line up close.
   b. Watch far enough ahead so that hazards can be anticipated.
   c. Follow the driver ahead closely and watch his brake lights.

42. In emergencies you may be able to miss an obstacle more quickly than you can stop. What is a characteristic of heavy vehicles when they are turned quickly?
   a. Top-heavy vehicles and tractors with multiple trailers cannot be turned quickly.
   b. Top-heavy vehicles and tractors with multiple trailers will unhook when turned quickly.
   c. Top-heavy vehicles and tractors with multiple trailers may flip over when turned quickly.

43. You are driving on a two-lane road when an oncoming driver drifts into your lane and is heading straight for you. What is one action to take?
   a. Braking while veering to the right when possible.
   b. Quickly turn to the left.
   c. Speed up to maneuver around the oncoming vehicle.

44. In making a quick turn what is a point to remember?
   a. Do not apply the brake when you are turning.
   b. The brakes will prevent skidding in turns.
   c. Do not expect to counter-steer.

45. What is controlled braking?
   a. Brake so that your wheels will stop rolling and bring the vehicle to a quick stop.
   b. Apply your brakes fully and do not release them.
   c. Applying the brakes as hard as you can without locking the wheels.

46. What is the major cause of most serious skids?
   a. Turning too sharply.
   b. Locking up the wheels.
   c. Driving too fast for road conditions.

47. What is the only way to stop a front wheel skid?
    a. Turn harder and brake harder.
    b. Stop turning and brake harder.
    c. Let the vehicle slow down. Stop turning and stop braking so hard.

48. If you think that a tire has blown out, what should you do in stopping?
    a. Hold the steering wheel firmly. Do not touch the brakes until the vehicle has slowed down when you can brake very gently.
    b. Hold the steering wheel firmly. Use hard braking to get off the highway as soon as possible and stop.
    c. Hold the steering wheel loosely. Use hard braking to stop.

49. What is something that you must do when using a fire extinguisher to fight a fire?
    a. Stay downwind.
    b. Aim at the base of the fire.
    c. Aim at the top of the fire.

50. As a driver for what are you responsible regarding your cargo?
    a. Inspecting your cargo, knowing that your cargo is securely tied down or covered, recognizing overloads and poorly balanced loads.
    b. Inspecting your cargo and keeping rainwater from getting under the pallets.
    c. Shifting your cargo at state lines and sliding your fifth wheel.

Answer Key

1. A
2. C
3. A
4. B
5. C
6. A
7. C
8. B
9. A
10. A
11. C
12. A
13. C
14. B
15. C
16. A
17. A
18. A
19. C
20. C
21. A
22. B
23. C
24. A
25. A
26. C
27. A
28. B
29. C
30. B
31. B
32. A
33. A
34. C
35. B
36. C
37. B
38. A
39. C
40. B
41. B
42. C
43. A
44. A
45. C
46. C
47. C
48. A
49. B
50. A

Air Brakes Endorsement

Air brakes

Air brakes use compressed air to make the brakes work. Air brakes are a good and safe way of stopping large and heavy vehicles, but the brakes must be well maintained and used properly. When we discuss air brakes, we are actually discussing three different braking systems. They are:

- Service brake - The service brake system applies and releases the brakes when you use the brake pedal during normal driving.
- Parking brake - The parking brake system applies and releases the parking brakes when you use the parking brake control. There are parking brakes for the truck and the trailer. When connected to a trailer, always set both brakes when parking.
- Emergency brake - The emergency brake system uses parts of the service and parking brake systems to stop the vehicle in a brake system failure.

Air brake system parts

Air compressor. The air compressor pumps air into the air storage tanks (reservoirs). The air compressor is connected to the engine through gears or a v-belt. The compressor may be air cooled or may be cooled by the engine cooling system. It may have its own oil supply or be lubricated by engine oil. If the compressor has its own oil supply, check the oil level before driving.

Air compressor governor. The governor controls when the air compressor will pump air into the air storage tanks. When air tank pressure rises to the "cut-out" level (around 125 pounds per-square-inch or "psi"), the governor stops the compressor from pumping air. When the tank pressure falls to the "cut-in" pressure (around 100 psi), the governor allows the compressor to start pumping again.

Air storage tanks: Air storage tanks are used to hold compressed air. The number and size of air tanks varies among vehicles. The tanks will hold enough air to allow the brakes to be used several times, even if the compressor stops working.

Air tank drains: Compressed air usually has some water and some compressor oil in it, which is bad for the air brake system. For example, the water can freeze in cold weather and cause brake failure. The water and oil tend to collect in the bottom of the air tank. Be sure that you drain the air tanks completely. Each air tank is equipped with a drain valve in the bottom. There are two types:

- Manually operated by turning a quarter turn or by pulling a cable. You must drain the tanks yourself at the end of each day of driving.
- Automatic--the water and oil are automatically expelled. These tanks may be equipped for manual draining as well. Automatic air tanks are available with electric heating devices. These help prevent freezing of the automatic drain in cold weather.

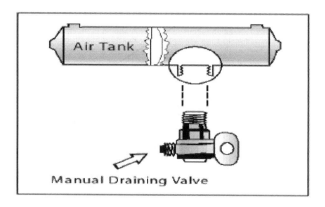

Alcohol evaporator: Some air brake systems have an alcohol evaporator to put alcohol into the air system. This helps to reduce the risk of ice in air brake valves and other parts during cold weather. Ice inside the system can make the brakes stop working. Check the alcohol container and fill up as necessary, every day during cold weather. Daily air tank drainage is still needed to get rid of water and oil. (Unless the system has automatic drain valves.)

Safety valve: A safety relief valve is installed in the first tank the air compressor pumps air to. The safety valve protects the tank and the rest of the system from too much pressure. The valve is usually set to open at 150 psi. If the safety valve releases air, something is wrong. Have the fault fixed by a mechanic.

The brake pedal: You put on the brakes by pushing down the brake pedal. (It is also called the foot valve or treadle valve.) Pushing the pedal down harder applies more air pressure. Letting up on the brake pedal reduces the air pressure and releases the brakes. Releasing the brakes lets some compressed air go out of the system, so the air pressure in the tanks is reduced. It must be made up by the air compressor. Pressing and releasing the pedal unnecessarily can let air out faster than the compressor can replace it. If the pressure gets too low, the brakes won't work.

Foundation brakes: Foundation brakes are used at each wheel. The most common type is the s-cam drum brake.

Brake drums, shoes, and linings: Brake drums are located on each end of the vehicle's axles. The wheels are bolted to the drums. The braking mechanism is inside the drum. To stop, the brake shoes and linings are pushed against the inside of the drum. This causes friction, which slows the vehicle (and creates heat). The heat a drum can take without damage depends on how hard and how long the brakes are used. Too much heat can make the brakes stop working.

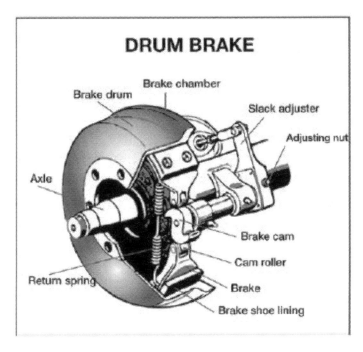

Supply pressure gauges: All vehicles with air brakes have a pressure gauge connected to the air tank. If the vehicle has a dual air brake system, there will be a gauge for each half of the system. (Or a single gauge with two needles.) Dual systems will be discussed later. These gauges tell you how much pressure is in the air tanks.

Application pressure gauge: This gauge shows you how much air pressure is being applied to the brakes. (This gauge is not on all vehicles.) Increasing application pressure to hold the same speed means the brakes are fading. You should slow down and use a lower gear. The need for increased pressure can also be caused by brakes out of adjustment, air leaks, or mechanical problems.

Low air pressure warning: A low air pressure warning signal is required on vehicles with air brakes. A warning signal you can see must come on before the air pressure in the tanks falls below 60 psi. (Or one half the compressor governor cutout pressure on older vehicles.) The warning is usually a red light. A buzzer may also come on.

Stop light switch: Drivers behind you must be warned when you put your brakes on. The air brake system does this with an electric switch that works by air pressure. The switch turns on the brake lights when you put on the air brakes.

Front brake limiting valve: Some older vehicles (made before 1975) have a front brake limiting valve and a control in the cab. The control is usually marked "normal" and "slippery." When you put the control in the "slippery" position, the limiting valve cuts the "normal" air pressure to the front brakes by half. Limiting valves were used to reduce the chance of the front wheels skidding on slippery surfaces. However, they actually reduce the stopping power of the vehicle. Front wheel braking is good under all conditions. Tests have shown front wheel skids from braking are not likely even on ice. Make sure the control is in the "Normal" position to have normal stopping power. Many vehicles have automatic front wheel limiting valves. They reduce the air to the front brakes except when the brakes are put on very hard (60 psi or more application pressure). These valves cannot be controlled by the driver.

Spring brakes: Many vehicles have automatic front wheel limiting valves. They reduce the air to the front brakes except when the brakes are put on very hard (60 psi or more application pressure). These valves cannot be controlled by the driver. Tractor and straight truck spring brakes will activate fully when air pressure drops to a range between 20 to 45 psi (typically 20 to 30 psi). Do not wait for the brakes to come on automatically. When the low air pressure warning light and buzzer first come on, bring the vehicle to a safe stop right away, while you still have control of the brakes. The braking power of spring brakes depends on the brakes being in adjustment. If the brakes are not adjusted properly, neither the regular brakes nor the emergency/parking brakes will work right.

Parking brake controls: In newer vehicles with air brakes, you put on the parking brakes using a diamond-shaped, yellow, push-pull control knob. You pull the knob out to put the parking brakes (spring brakes) on, and push it in to release them. On older vehicles, the parking brakes may be controlled by a lever. Use the parking brakes whenever you park.

Never push the brake pedal down when the spring brakes are on. If you do, the brakes could be damaged by the combined forces of the springs and the air pressure. Many brake systems are designed in a way that will not allow this to happen. However, not all systems are set up that way, and those that are may not always work.

Modulating control valves: In some vehicles a control handle on the dash board may be used to apply the spring brakes gradually. This is called a modulating valve. It is spring-loaded so you have a feel for the braking action. The more you move the control lever, the harder the spring brakes come on. They work this way so you can control the spring brakes if the service brakes fail. When parking a vehicle with a modulating control valve, move the lever as far as it will go and hold it in place with the locking device.

Dual parking control valves: When main air pressure is lost, the spring brakes come on. Some vehicles, such as buses, have a separate air tank which can be used to release the spring brakes. This is so you can move the vehicle in an emergency. One of the valves is a push-pull type and is used to put on the spring brakes for parking. The other valve is spring loaded in the "out" position. When you push the control in, air from the separate air tank releases the spring brakes so you can move. When you release the button, the spring brakes come on again. There is only enough air in the separate tank to do this a few times. Therefore, plan carefully when moving. Otherwise, you may be stopped in a dangerous location when the separate air supply runs out. Use the parking brakes whenever you park.

Antilock Braking Systems (ABS): Truck tractors with air brakes built on or after March 1, 1997, and other air brakes vehicles, (trucks, buses, trailers, and converter dollies) built on or after March 1, 1998, are required to be equipped with antilock brakes. Many commercial vehicles built before these dates have been voluntarily equipped with ABS. Check the certification label for the date of manufacture to determine if your vehicle is equipped with ABS. ABS is a computerized system that keeps your wheels from locking up during hard brake applications. Vehicles with ABS have yellow malfunction lamps to tell you if something isn't working. Tractors, trucks, and buses will have yellow ABS malfunction lamps on the instrument panel. Trailers will have yellow ABS malfunction lamps on the left side, either on the front or rear corner. Dollies manufactured on or after March 1, 1998 are required to have a lamp on the left side.

On newer vehicles, the malfunction lamp comes on at start-up for a bulb check, and then goes out quickly. On older systems, the lamp could stay on until you are driving over five mph. If the lamp stays on after the bulb check, or goes on once you are under way, you may have lost ABS control at one or more wheels. In the case of towed units manufactured before it was required by the Department of Transportation, it may be difficult to tell if the unit is equipped with ABS. Look under the vehicle for the electronic control unit (ECU) and wheel speed sensor wires coming from the back of the brakes. ABS is an addition to your normal brakes. It does not decrease or increase your normal braking capability. ABS only activates when wheels are about to lock up. ABS does not necessarily shorten your stopping distance, but it does help you keep the vehicle under control during hard braking.

Dual air brake systems

Most heavy-duty vehicles use dual air brake systems for safety. A dual air brake system has two separate air brake systems, which use a single set of brake controls. Each system has its own air tanks, hoses, lines, etc. One system typically operates the regular brakes on the rear axle or axles. The other system operates the regular brakes on the front axle (and possibly one rear axle). Both systems supply air to the trailer (if there is one). The first system is called the "primary" system. The other is called the "secondary" system. Before driving a vehicle with a dual air system, allow time for the air compressor to build up a minimum of 100 psi pressure in both the primary and secondary systems. Watch the primary and secondary air pressure gauges (or needles, if the system has two needles in one gauge). Pay attention to the low air pressure warning light and buzzer. The warning light and buzzer should shut off when air pressure in both systems rises to a value set by the manufacturer. This value must be greater than 60 psi. The warning light and buzzer should come on before the air pressure drops below 60 psi in either system. If this happens while driving, you should stop right away and safely park the vehicle. If one air system is very low on pressure, either the front or the rear brakes will not be operating fully. This means it will take you longer to stop. Bring the vehicle to a safe stop, and have the air brakes system fixed.

Inspecting air brake systems

There are more things to inspect on a vehicle with air brakes than one without them:
- Engine compartment check
    - Check the air compressor drive belt if the compressor is belt driven. Check the condition and tightness of the belt.
- Walk-around inspection
    - Check the manual slack adjusters on the S-Cam brakes.
    - Park on level ground and chock the wheels.
    - Turn off the parking brakes so you can move the slack adjusters.
    - Use gloves and pull hard on each slack adjuster that you can reach.
    - If a slack adjuster moves more than about one inch where the push rod attaches to it, it probably needs adjustment.
    - Adjust it or have it adjusted. Vehicles with too much brake slack can be hard to stop. Out-of-adjustment brakes are the most common problem found in roadside inspections.
    - Check the brake drums (or discs), linings and hoses.
    - Brake drums or discs cannot have cracks longer than half the width of the friction area.
    - Linings (friction material) cannot be loose, soaked with oil or grease. They cannot be dangerously thin.
    - Mechanical parts must be in place and should not be broken or missing.
    - Check the air hoses connected to the brake chambers to make sure they are not cut or worn due to rubbing.
- Check the air brake system.
    - Checking the air brake system is different from the hydraulic brake check shown in Section 1: General Knowledge.
        - Test the low pressure warning signal.
        - Shut off the engine when you have enough air pressure so that the low pressure warning signal is off.
        - Turn on the electrical power and step on and off the brake pedal to reduce air tank pressure.
        - The low air pressure warning signal must come on before the pressure drops to less than 60 psi in the air tank (or tank with the lowest air pressure in dual air systems).
        - If the warning signal doesn't work, you could lose air pressure without knowing it. This could cause sudden emergency braking. In dual systems, the stopping distance will be increased. Only limited breaking can be done before the spring brakes come on.
    - Be sure that spring brakes come on automatically.
        - Chock the wheels, release the parking brakes when you have enough air pressure and shut off the engine.
        - Step on and off the brake pedal to reduce the air tank pressure.
        - The parking brake knob should pop out when the air pressure falls to the manufacturer's specification (usually between 20 and 40 psi). This causes the spring brakes to come on.
        - Check the rate of air pressure build-up.
        - When the engine is at operating RPM (check the manufacturer's specifications to determine the correct operating RPM), the pressure should build from 85 to 100 psi within 45 seconds in dual air systems.
        - If the vehicle has larger than minimum air tanks, the buildup time can be longer. Check the manufacturer's specifications.
        - In single air systems (built before 1975), pressure typically builds from 50 to 90 psi within 3 minutes with the engine at an idle speed of 600-900 RPM.

- If air pressure does not build fast enough, your pressure may drop too low during driving. This will require an emergency stop. Don't drive until you get the problem fixed.
  o Test the air leakage rate.
    - When the air system is fully charged (between 120 and 125 psi), turn off the engine, release the service brake and time the air pressure drop. The loss rate should be less than 2 psi in one minute for single vehicles. It should be less than 3 psi in one minute for combination vehicles.
    - Apply 90 psi or more with the brake pedal. After the initial pressure drop, if air pressure falls more than 3 psi in one minute for single vehicles (4 psi for combination vehicles), the air loss rate is too high.
    - Check for air leaks and fix them before driving or you could lose your brakes while driving.
  o Check the air compressor governor cut-in and cut-out pressures.
    - Air compressor pumping should start at about 100 psi and stop at about 125 psi. Check the manufacturer's specifications.
    - Run the engine at a fast idle. The air governor should cut out the air compressor at the manufacturer's specified pressure. The air pressure shown by your gauge(s) will stop rising.
    - With the engine idling, step on and off the brake to reduce the air tank pressure. The compressor should cut in at the manufacturer's specified cut-in pressure. The pressure should begin to rise.
    - If the air governor does not work as described above, it may need to be fixed. A governor that does not work right may not keep enough air pressure for safe driving.
  o Test the parking brake. Stop the vehicle, put on the parking brake and gently pull against it in a low gear to test that the parking brake will hold.
  o Test the service brakes.
    - Wait for normal air pressure to build, release the parking brake, move the vehicle forward slowly (about 5 mph) and apply the brakes firmly using the brake pedal.
    - Watch to see if the vehicle pulls to one side, feels unusual or stops slowly.
    - This test can show you problems which you would not know about until you used the brakes on the road.

Using air brakes

Normal stops
Push the brake pedal down. Control the pressure so the vehicle comes to a smooth, safe stop. If you have a manual transmission, don't push the clutch in until the engine rpm is down close to idle. When stopped, select a starting gear.

Braking with antilock brakes
When you brake hard on slippery surfaces in a vehicle without ABS, your wheels may lock up. When your steering wheels lock up, you lose steering control. When your other wheels lock up, you may skid, jackknife, or even spin the vehicle. ABS helps you avoid wheel lock up. The computer senses impending lockup, reduces the braking pressure to a safe level, and you maintain control. You may or may not be able to stop faster with ABS, but you should be able to steer around an obstacle while braking, and avoid skids caused by over braking. Having ABS on only the tractor, only the trailer, or even on only one axle, still gives you more control over the vehicle during braking. Brake normally. When only the tractor has ABS, you should be able to maintain steering control, and there is less chance of jackknifing. But, keep your eye on the trailer and let up on the brakes (if you can safely do so) if it begins to swing out. When only the trailer has ABS, the trailer is less likely to swing out, but if you lose steering control or start a tractor

jackknife, let up on the brakes (if you can safely do so) until you gain control. When you drive a tractor-trailer combination with ABS, you should brake as you always have. In other words:

- Use only the braking force necessary to stop safely and stay in control.
- Brake the same way, regardless of whether you have ABS on the tractor, the trailer, or both.
- As you slow down, monitor your tractor and trailer and back off the brakes (if it is safe to do so) to stay in control.

There is only one exception to this procedure, if you always drive a straight truck or combination with working ABS on all axles, in an emergency stop, you can fully apply the brakes. Without ABS, you still have normal brake functions. Drive and brake as you always have. Remember, if your ABS malfunctions, you still have regular brakes. Drive normally, but get the system serviced soon.

Braking on downgrades

The use of brakes on a long and/or steep downgrade is only a supplement to the braking effect of the engine. Once the vehicle is in the proper low gear, the following is the proper braking technique:

- Apply the brakes just hard enough to feel a definite slowdown.
- When your speed has been reduced to approximately five mph below your "safe" speed, release the brakes. (This application should last for about three seconds.)
- When your speed has increased to your "safe" speed, repeat steps 1 and 2.

For example, if your "safe" speed is 40 mph, you would not apply the brakes until your speed reaches 40 mph. You now apply the brakes hard enough to gradually reduce your speed to 35 mph and then release the brakes. Repeat this as often as necessary until you have reached the end of the downgrade.

Stopping distance

Air brakes increase your stopping distance. Hydraulic brakes (used on cars and light/medium trucks) work instantly. Air brakes take half a second or more for the air to flow through the lines to the brakes. Due to this, vehicles with air brakes require more stopping distance than vehicles with other types of brakes. The total stopping distance for vehicles with air brake systems is made up of four different factors:

- Perception distance - the distance your vehicle travels from the time your eyes see a hazard until your brain recognizes it.
- Reaction distance - the distance your vehicle travels from the time your brain tells your foot to move from the accelerator until the time your foot pushes the brake.
- Brake lag distance - the distance your vehicle travels from the time your foot pushes the air brake until the brake takes hold.
- Braking distance - the distance your vehicle travels between the time the brakes take hold and the vehicle stops.

By adding these distances together, you will get your total stopping distance. The air brake lag distance at 55 mph on dry pavement adds about 32 feet. So at 55 mph for an average driver under good traction and brake conditions, the total stopping distance is over 450 feet.

Brake fading or failure

Brakes are designed so brake shoes or pads rub against the brake drum or disks to slow the vehicle. Braking creates heat, but brakes are designed to take a lot of heat. However, brakes can fade or fail from excessive heat caused by using them too much and not relying on the engine braking effect. Excessive use of the service brakes causes overheating and leads to brake fade. Excessive heat in the brakes causes chemical changes in the lining which reduces friction and causes the brake drums to expand. As the overheated drums expand, the brake shoes and linings have to move farther to contact the drums, and the force of this contact is reduced.

Continued overuse may increase brake fade until the vehicle cannot be slowed down or stopped. Brake fade is also affected by adjustment. To safely control a vehicle, every brake must do its share of the work. Brakes out of adjustment will stop doing their share before those that are in adjustment. The other brakes can then overheat and fade, and there will not be enough braking available to control the vehicle(s). Brakes can get out of adjustment quickly, especially when they are hot. Therefore, check brake adjustment often.

Low air pressure

If the low air pressure warning comes on, stop and safely park your vehicle as soon as possible. There might be an air leak in the system. Controlled braking is possible only while enough air remains in the air tanks. The spring brakes will come on when the air pressure drops into the range of 20 to 45 psi. A heavily loaded vehicle will take a long distance to stop because the spring brakes do not work on all axles. Lightly loaded vehicles or vehicles on slippery roads may skid out of control when the spring brakes come on. It is much safer to stop while there is enough air in the tanks to use the foot brakes.

Parking brakes

Any time you park, use the parking brakes, except as noted below. Pull the parking brake control knob out to apply the parking brakes, push it in to release. The control will be a yellow, diamond-shaped knob labeled "parking brakes" on newer vehicles. On older vehicles, it may be a round blue knob or some other shape (including a lever that swings from side to side or up and down). Don't use the parking brakes if the brakes are very hot (from just having come down a steep grade), or if the brakes are very wet in freezing temperatures. If they are used while they are very hot, they can be damaged by the heat. If they are used in freezing temperatures when the brakes are very wet, they can freeze so the vehicle cannot move. Use wheel chocks on a level surface to hold the vehicle. Let hot brakes cool before using the parking brakes. If the brakes are wet, use the brakes lightly while driving in a low gear to heat and dry them. If your vehicle does not have automatic air tank drains, drain your air tanks at the end of each working day to remove moisture and oil. Otherwise, the brakes could fail. Never leave your vehicle unattended without applying the parking brakes or chocking the wheels. The vehicle could roll, causing injury and damage.

Airbrakes Endorsement Tests

Part One

1. What are the three braking systems?
    a. The parking brake and emergency brake and thermal system
    b. The service brake and parking brake and emergency system.
    c. The service brake and emergency and the inverse system.

2. What is used to make the brakes work?
    a. Compressed Oxygen.
    b. Compressed Nitrogen.
    c. Compressed air.

3. What does the air compressor do?
    a. Pumps air into the air storage tanks.
    b. Keeps the tires inflated to proper pressure
    c. Comes on only if you have to make an emergency stop.

4. What does the air compressor governor control?
    a. It controls emergency warning systems.
    b. It controls when the compressor will pump air into the air storage tanks.
    c. It controls how the compressor will pump air into the air lines.

5. How much compressed air must the storage tanks hold?
    a. At least one hundred and twenty pounds of air.
    b. A maximum of one atmosphere.
    c. Enough air to allow brakes to be used when the air compressor stops working.

6. If oil and water collect in the air tanks what can happen to the brakes?
    a. The brakes can fail.
    b. Brake linings will automatically slip loose
    c. The brakes will work better.

7. No automatic tank drains - when should you drain the air tanks?
    a. Once a week.
    b. Once a month.
    c. Every day.

8. Where will you find the drain valve for each air tank?
    a. In the bottom of the tank.
    b. At the top of the tank.
    c. It is usually found above the tank.

9. What are the two types of air tank drains?
    a. Manually operated. . . Emergency.
    b. Automatic . . . Emergency.
    c. Manually operated. . . Automatic.

10. What is a purpose of an alcohol evaporator?
    a. It takes alcohol from the air system.
    b. It reduces risk of ice in brake valves and other parts in cold weather.
    c. It is designed to save fuel in warm weather.

Part Two

1. How often should you check the alcohol evaporator in cold weather?
    a. Check the alcohol container and fill up as necessary once each week.
    b. Check the alcohol container once each fall before cold weather starts.
    c. Check the alcohol container and fill up as necessary every day.

2. What is a purpose of the safety release valve in the first tank?
    a. It protects the tank and the rest of the system from too much pressure
    b. It protects all of the system from dirt and oil.
    c. It helps build up air pressure quickly without running the engine.

3. What are two other names for the brake pedal?
    a. It can be called the foot valve or the relay valve.
    b. It can be called the foot valve or treadle valve.
    c. It can be called the relay valve or air compressor valve.

4. What can happen if the brake pedal is pressed and released too often?
    a. The brakes will be cooled down as soon as all the hot air is removed.
    b. Air pressure can build up until the brake pressure gauge is broken.
    c. Air can be let out of the system faster than the compressor can replace.

5. Where are foundation brakes found?
    a. At each wheel.
    b. On every other axle.
    c. On the drive wheels only.

6. Where are brake shoes and linings located?
    a. Directly beneath the foot valve.
    b. Inside each brake drum
    c. On the outside of certain brake drums.

7. What happens when a brake lining is pushed against the inside of the drum?
    a. The brakes will always squeal.
    b. This causes friction which slows the vehicle and creates heat.
    c. This causes heat which automatically causes the brakes to lock up.

8. On S-Cam brakes what happens to the air when you push the brake pedal?
    a. Air pressure forces out the push rod and moves the slack adjuster.
    b. Air pressure works only with wedge brakes and not with S-Cam brakes.
    c. Air pressure is converted into hydraulic pressure.

9. Which direction does the S-Cam force brake shoes when brakes are applied?
    a. It presses them against the outside of the brake drum.
    b. It presses them against the inside of the brake drum.
    c. It presses them around the brake drum.

10. If the air compressor begins to leak what keeps air in the tanks?
    a. The slack adjusters.
    b. The alcohol evaporator.
    c. The one-way check valve.

Part Three

1. What is one kind of gauge that is required for vehicles with air brakes?
    a. An air temperature gauge.
    b. An air pressure gauge
    c. An oil pressure gauge.

2. What kind of warning signal is required on vehicles with air brakes?
    a. A high air pressure warning signal.
    b. A low air pressure warning signal.
    c. A changing air pressure warning signal.

3. What are the three types of low air pressure warning devices?
    a. A siren . . . or a horn . . . or 4-way flashers.
    b. A red light . . . or a buzzer . . . or a wigwag.
    c. An air horn . . . or an amber light . . . or a whistle.

4. What is used to turn on the stop lights in an air brakes system?
    a. An electric switch that works by air pressure
    b. A computer.
    c. A motion sensor in the wheels.

5. In normal driving parking and emergency brakes are usually held back by?
    a. Electric relay switches.
    b. Wheel chocks.
    c. Air pressure.

6. The effectiveness of the spring brakes depends on the adjustment of?
    a. Emergency brakes.
    b. Service brakes.
    c. Front wheel brakes.

7. Why do some buses have a separate air tank to release spring brakes?
    a. So you can move the vehicle in an emergency.
    b. To simplify servicing the air brake system.
    c. So that the brakes will release quicker.

8. What is a dual air brake system?
    a. Two separate air brake systems with a single set of brake controls.
    b. One air brake system with two sets of brake controls.
    c. Two separate air brake systems with two sets of brake controls.

9. What should you look for in checking an air compressor belt?
    a. Check for belts that are the wrong color.
    b. Check for belts that are not made of rubber.
    c. Check belts for excessive wear and cracks and tightness.

10. What should you do before checking free play in manual slack adjusters?
    a. Park in a secure location and remove all wheel chocks.
    b. Park on level ground so that the wheels will not have to be chocked.
    c. Park on level ground and chock the wheels and release parking brakes.

Part Four

1. Combination vehicle: brakes released. The maximum air released?
    a. One pound per square inch.
    b. Less than two pounds per square inch
    c. Less than three pounds per square inch.

2. Single vehicle: brakes released. Maximum air leakage in one minute?
    a. One pound per square inch.
    b. Less than two pounds per square inch.
    c. Less than three pounds per square inch.

3. After applying brakes fully, maximum air loss in one minute - single vehicles?
    a. Two pounds per square inch.
    b. Three pounds per square inch.
    c. Four pounds per square inch.

4. After applying brakes fully max. air loss in one minute - combination vehicles?
    a. Two pounds per square inch.
    b. Three pounds per square inch.
    c. Four pounds per square inch.

5. When should the air governor cut out the air compressor?
    a. At about the manufacturer specified air pressure.
    b. At about ten pounds per square inch.
    c. At about one hundred and ten pounds per square inch.

6. When making a normal stop when should you push in the clutch?
    a. Experienced drivers do not use the clutch.
    b. Do not push in the clutch until there is vibration.
    c. Do not push the clutch in until the engine R.P.M.'s are down close to idle.

7. When making a very quick stop you should brake so that you?
    a. Can turn quickly to get out the way of hazards.
    b. Skid to maximize stopping distance.
    c. Stay in a straight line and can steer.

8. What is another name for controlled braking?
    a. Steady braking.
    b. Hard braking.
    c. Squeeze braking.

9. What is stab braking?
    a. Putting the brakes on hard without locking the wheels or turning
    b. Pressing the brake pedal hard and releasing brakes when wheels lock up.
    c. Applying a constant pressure to the brakes.

10. Why does air braking take more time than hydraulic braking?
    a. Because air brakes are generally used on longer vehicles
    b. Because it takes time for air to flow through the lines to the brakes.
    c. Because air moves through the lines much slower than oil does.

Answer Key

Part One

1. B: The service brake and parking brake and emergency system.
2. C: Compressed air.
3. A: Pumps air into the air storage tanks.
4. B: It controls when the compressor will pump air into the air storage tanks.
5. C: Enough air to allow brakes to be used when the air compressor stops working.
6. A: The brakes can fail.
7. C: Every day.
8. A: In the bottom of the tank.
9. C: Manually operated. . . Automatic.
10. B: It reduces risk of ice in brake valves and other parts in cold weather.

Part Two

1. C: Check the alcohol container and fill up as necessary every day.
2. A: It protects the tank and the rest of the system from too much pressure
3. B: It can be called the foot valve or treadle valve.
4. C: Air can be let out of the system faster than the compressor can replace.
5. A: At each wheel.
6. B: Inside each brake drum
7. B: This causes friction which slows the vehicle and creates heat.
8. A: Air pressure forces out the push rod and moves the slack adjuster.
9. B: It presses them against the inside of the brake drum.
10. C: The one-way check valve.

Part Three

1. B: An air pressure gauge
2. B: A low air pressure warning signal.
3. B: A red light . . . or a buzzer . . . or a wigwag.
4. A: An electric switch that works by air pressure
5. C: Air pressure.
6. B: Service brakes.
7. A: So you can move the vehicle in an emergency.
8. A: Two separate air brake systems with a single set of brake controls.
9. C: Check belts for excessive wear and cracks and tightness.
10. C: Park on level ground and chock the wheels and release parking brakes.

Part Four

1. C: Less than three pounds per square inch.
2. B: Less than two pounds per square inch.
3. B: Three pounds per square inch.
4. C: Four pounds per square inch.
5. A: At about the manufacturer specified air pressure.
6. C: Do not push the clutch in until the engine R.P.M.'s are down close to idle.
7. C: Stay in a straight line and can steer.
8. C: Squeeze braking.
9. B: Pressing the brake pedal hard and releasing brakes when wheels lock up.
10. B: Because it takes time for air to flow through the lines to the brakes.

Cargo and Transport Vehicles Endorsement

This section covers hauling cargo safely. You must first understand basic cargo safety rules to get a CDL. Cargo that is loaded poorly, or that is not secured, is a danger to yourself and others. Loose cargo can:
- Fall from the vehicle and cause a crash;
- Hurt or kill you if you stop quickly or crash;
- Make it difficult for you to steer the vehicle.

Additionally, loose cargo can be damaged by sliding back and forth and can damage the vehicle. You may load and secure the cargo yourself or someone else may load and secure it. In either case, you must:
- Inspect the cargo, unless it is a sealed load or the manner of handling makes inspection impractical.
- Recognize overloads and poorly balanced weight.
- Ensure that the cargo is properly secured.

If you plan to carry hazardous materials that will require placards on your vehicle, you must have a hazardous materials endorsement. You must also be at least 21 years of age.

Cargo weight and balance

Definitions of Weight:
Gross vehicle weight (GVW) The total weight of a single vehicle plus the cargo.
Gross combination weight (GCW) The total weight of a powered unit (tractor) plus the trailer or trailers plus the cargo.
Gross vehicle weight rating (GVWR) The maximum GVW specified by the manufacturer for a single vehicle plus the cargo (maximum scale weight).
Axle weight The weight transferred to the ground by one axle or one set of axles.

Legal weight limits

You must keep weights within legal limits. States have maximums for GVWs, GCWs, and axle weights. Often, maximum axle weights are set by a bridge formula. A bridge formula permits less maximum axle weight for axles that are closer together. This is to prevent overloading bridges and roadways.

Overloading affects safety

Overloading can have bad effects on steering, braking, and speed control. Overloaded trucks have to go very slowly on upgrades. Worse, they may gain too much speed on downgrades. Stopping distance increases. Brakes can fail when forced to work too hard. During bad weather or in mountains, it may not be safe to operate at legal maximum weights. Take this into account before driving.

69

Don't be top heavy

The height of the vehicle's center of gravity is very important for safe handling. A high center of gravity (cargo piled up high or heavy cargo on top) means you are more likely to tip over. It is most dangerous in curves, or if you have to swerve to avoid a hazard. It is very important to distribute the cargo so it is as low as possible. Put the heaviest parts of the cargo under the lightest parts.

Balance the weight

Poor weight balance can make vehicle handling unsafe. Too much weight on the steering axle can cause hard steering. It can damage the steering axle and tires. Under-loaded front axles (caused by shifting weight too far to the rear) can make the steering axle weight too light to steer safely. Too little weight on the driving axles can cause poor traction. The drive wheels may spin easily. During bad weather, the truck may not be able to keep going. Weight that is loaded so there is a high center of gravity causes greater chance of rollover. On flat bed vehicles, there is also a greater chance that the load will shift to the side or fall off.

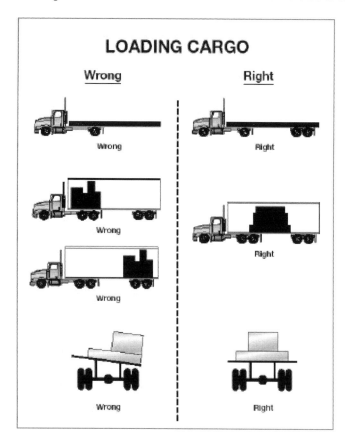

Securing cargo

Blocking
Blocking is used in the front, back, and/or sides of a piece of cargo to keep it from sliding. Blocking is shaped to fit snugly against cargo. It is secured to the cargo deck to prevent cargo movement.

Bracing
Bracing is also used to prevent movement of cargo. Bracing goes from the upper part of the cargo to the floor and/or walls of the cargo compartment.

Cargo tiedowns

On flatbed trailers or trailers without sides, cargo must be secured to keep it from shifting or falling off. In closed vans, tiedowns can also be important to prevent cargo shifting that may affect the handling of the vehicle. Tiedowns must be of the proper type and proper strength. Federal regulations require the aggregate working load limit of any securement system used to secure an article or group of articles against movement must be at least one-half times the weight of the article or group of articles. Proper tiedown equipment must be used, including ropes, straps, chains, and tensioning devices (winches, ratchets, clinching components). Tiedowns must be attached to the vehicle correctly (hooks, bolts, rails, rings). Cargo should have at least one tiedown for each ten feet of cargo. Make sure you have enough tiedowns to meet this need. No matter how small the cargo, it should have at least two tiedowns.

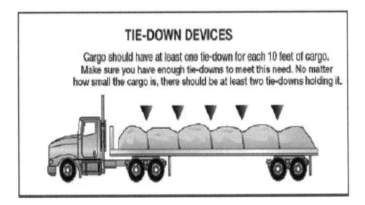

There are special requirements for securing various heavy pieces of metal. Find out what they are if you have to carry such loads.

Header boards

Front-end header boards ("headache racks") protect you from your cargo in case of a crash or emergency stop. Make sure the front-end structure is in good condition. The front-end structure should block the forward movement of any cargo you carry.

Covering cargo

There are two basic reasons for covering cargo:
- To protect people from spilled cargo.
- To protect the cargo from weather.

Spill protection is a safety requirement in many states. Be familiar with the laws in the states you drive in. You should look at your cargo covers in the mirrors from time to time while driving. A flapping cover can tear loose, uncovering the cargo, and possibly block your view or someone else's.

Sealed and containerized loads

Containerized loads generally are used when freight is carried part way by rail or ship. Delivery by truck occurs at the beginning and/or end of the journey. Some containers have their own tiedown devices or locks that attach directly to a special frame. Others have to be loaded onto flat bed trailers. They must be properly secured just like any other cargo. You cannot inspect sealed loads, but you should check that you don't exceed gross weight and axle weight limits.

Other cargo

Hanging meat
Hanging meat (suspended beef, pork, lamb) in a refrigerated truck can be a very unstable load with a high center of gravity. Particular caution is needed on sharp curves such as off ramps and on ramps. Go slowly.

Livestock
Livestock can move around in a trailer, causing unsafe handling. With less than a full load, use false bulkheads to keep livestock bunched together. Even when bunched, special care is necessary because livestock can lean on curves. This shifts the center of gravity and makes rollover more likely.

Over-length, over-width and/or over-weight loads
Over-length, over-width and/or over-weight loads require special transit permits. Driving is usually limited to certain times. Special equipment may be necessary such as "wide load" signs, flashing lights, flags, etc. Such loads may require a police escort or pilot vehicles bearing warning signs and/or flashing lights. These special loads require special driving care. Check with each state you plan to travel through for specific requirements.

Dry bulk tanks
Dry bulk tanks require special care because they have a high center of gravity, and the load can shift. Be extremely cautious (slow and careful) going around curves and making sharp turns.

Tank Vehicles Endorsement

A tank endorsement is required for certain vehicles that transport liquids or gases. The liquid or gas does not have to be a hazardous material. A tank endorsement is required if your vehicle needs a Class A or B CDL and you want to haul a liquid or liquid gas in a permanently mounted cargo tank rated at 119 gallons or more or a portable tank rated at 1,000 gallons or more. A tank endorsement is also required for Class C vehicles when the vehicle is used to transport hazardous materials in liquid or gas form in the above described rated tanks. Before loading, unloading, or driving a tanker, inspect the vehicle. This makes sure that the vehicle is safe to carry the liquid or gas and is safe to drive.

Inspecting tank vehicles

Tank vehicles have special items that you need to check. Tank vehicles come in many types and sizes. You need to check the vehicle's operator manual to make sure you know how to inspect your tank vehicle. On all tank vehicles, the most important item to check for is leaks. Check under and around the vehicle for signs of any leaking. Don't carry liquids or gases in a leaking tank. To do so is a crime. You will be cited and prevented from driving further. You may also be liable for the cleanup of any spill. In general, check the following:

- Check the tank's body or shell for dents or leaks.
- Check the intake, discharge and cut-off valves. Make sure the valves are in the correct position before loading, unloading or moving the vehicle.
- Check pipes, connections, and hoses for leaks, especially around joints.
- Check manhole covers and vents. Make sure the covers have gaskets and they close correctly. Keep the vents clear so they work correctly.
- Check special purpose equipment. If your vehicle has any one of the following equipment, make sure it works:
  - Vapor recovery kits
  - Grounding and bonding cables
  - Emergency shut-off systems
  - Built-in fire extinguisher

Never drive a tank vehicle with open valves or manhole covers. Check the emergency equipment required for your vehicle. Find out what equipment you are required to carry and make sure you have it and know how it works.

Driving tank vehicles

Hauling liquids in tanks requires special skills because of the vehicle's high center of gravity and liquid movement.

- Tank vehicles have a high center of gravity. High center of gravity means that much of the load's weight is carried high up off the road. This makes the vehicle top-heavy and easy to roll over. Liquid tankers are especially easy to roll over. Tests have shown that tankers can turn over at the speed limits posted for curves. Take highway curves and on ramp/off ramp curves well below the posted speeds.
- Watch out for liquid surge. Liquid surge results from movement of the liquid in partially filled tanks. This movement can have bad effects on handling. For example, when coming to a stop, the liquid will surge back and forth. When the wave hits the end of the tank, it tends to push the truck in the direction the wave is moving. If the truck is on a slippery surface such as ice, the wave can shove a stopped truck out into an intersection. The driver of a liquid tanker must be very familiar with the handling of the vehicle.
- Bulkheads. Some liquid tanks are divided into several smaller tanks by bulkheads. When loading and unloading the smaller tanks, the driver must pay attention to weight distribution. Don't put too much weight on the front or rear of the vehicle.
- Baffled tanks. Baffled liquid tanks have bulkheads in them with holes that let the liquid flow through. The baffles help to control the forward and backward liquid surge. Side-to-side surge can still occur. This can cause a roll over.
- Un-baffled tanks. Un-baffled liquid tankers (sometimes called "smooth bore" tanks) have nothing inside to slow down the flow of the liquid. Therefore, forward-and-back surge is very strong. Un-baffled tanks are usually those that transport food products (milk, for example). (Sanitation regulations forbid the use of baffles because of the difficulty in cleaning the inside of the tank.) Be extremely cautious (slow and careful) in driving smooth bore tanks, especially when starting and stopping.
- Outage. Never load a cargo tank totally full. Liquids expand as they warm. This is called outage. You must leave room for the liquid to expand. Different liquids expand by different amounts and require different amounts of outage. You must know the outage requirement for the liquids that you haul.
- How much to load? A full tank of dense liquid, such as some acids, may exceed legal weight limits. Therefore, you may often only partially fill tanks with heavy liquids. The amount of liquid that you can load into a tank depends on:
  - Amount that the liquid will expand in transit;
  - Weight of the liquid; and,
  - Legal weight limits.

Safe driving rules

The following are rules for safe driving:

- Drive smoothly. Because of the high center of gravity and the surge of the liquid, you must start, slow down, and stop very smoothly. Make smooth turns and lane changes.
- Use controlled or stab braking. If you must stop quickly to avoid a crash, use controlled or stab braking. Also, remember that if you steer quickly while braking, your vehicle may roll over. Always wear your seatbelt.
- Slow down before curves. Slow down before curves, then accelerate slightly through the curve. The posted speed for a curve may be too fast for a tank vehicle.
- Maintain a safe stopping distance between you and the vehicle ahead. Keep in mind how much space you need to stop your vehicle. Remember that wet roads double the normal stopping distance. Empty tank vehicles may take longer to stop than full ones.
- Skids. Don't over steer, over accelerate, or over brake. If you do, your vehicle may skid. On tank trailers, if your drive wheels or trailer wheels begin to skid, your vehicle may jackknife. When any vehicle starts to skid, you must take action to restore traction to the wheels.

Cargo and Tank Endorsement Tests

Part One

1. A 'tank vehicle' includes?
    a. Portable tanks having a capacity of 100 gallons or more
    b. Dry bulk tank vehicles
    c. Transit mix trucks and cement mixers

2. With tank vehicles 'Outage' means?
    a. An electrical failure when the engine is shut off
    b. Sparks that fly up from the pavement when touched by a ground wire
    c. Space that must be left in a cargo tank for liquids to expand

3. Why should you find out the 'Outage' for the liquids you are transporting?
    a. Different liquids expand by different amounts.
    b. You cannot operate a tank if the electrical system is not working.
    c. A liquid that has frozen is no longer considered to be a liquid.

4. What are two problems especially important to tanker operation?
    a. A high center of gravity and the liquid surge of the cargo transported
    b. A low center of gravity and leakage from tanks
    c. The tendency of milk to spoil and driver inability to see into the tank

5. What is a tank compartment?
    a. A tank for storing hoses and couplings
    b. A liquid-tight division of a tank
    c. A wall with many openings

6. How is a bulkhead different from a baffle?
    a. Bulkheads are larger than baffles.
    b. Bulkheads are liquid-tight and baffles have holes in them.
    c. Bulkheads are placed vertically while baffles are horizontal.

7. Which is a factor that determines the amount of liquid you can load in a tank?
    a. The failure of molasses to flow properly in cold weather
    b. The height of the tractor
    c. The weight of the liquid

8. One of these helps determine the amount of liquid you can load in a tank.
    a. The legal weight and load limits of your vehicle
    b. The wheelbase between your front and second axles
    c. The number of pumps that can be used to load your tank

9. Which of these helps determine the amount of liquid you can load in a tank?
    a. The size of the opening in the dome lid
    b. The amount that the liquid might expand in transit
    c. The maximum speed at which you will be driving

10. Why is the danger of liquid surge more when a tank is less than full?
    a. Liquid has more room to move in a partially-filled tank.
    b. The air pressure is greater inside a partially-filled tank.
    c. Many semi trailer tanks are slanted so that the lower end is at the back.

Part Two

1. The side-to-side surge of liquid in a tank can cause a vehicle to?
   a. Stop instantly
   b. Bend at the fifth wheel connection
   c. Roll over

2. Do the speed limits posted for on-ramps and off-ramps apply to tankers?
   a. Yes, all limits are set with tankers in mind.
   b. No, tankers are exempt.
   c. Not necessarily

3. Are smooth bore tankers different to drive than tankers with tank baffles?
   a. No, except that smooth bore tanks usually transport food products.
   b. Yes, forward and back surge is strong in smooth bore tankers.
   c. No, but tanks with bulkheads or baffles are harder to keep clean.

4. Baffles offer little resistance to?
   a. Front-to-back surge
   b. Back-to-front surge
   c. Side-to-side surge

5. In what direction does liquid surge cause a vehicle to move?
   a. Forward and much faster
   b. Backward and much slower
   c. It will tend to move the vehicle in the direction that the liquid moves.

6. As compared to a smooth bore tank, a tank with bulkheads or baffles?
   a. Will have less front-to-back surge
   b. Will have less side-to-side surge
   c. There will be no difference.

7. Why are unbaffled tanks used to transport food products?
   a. Sanitation regulations often forbid the use of baffles.
   b. Food products are lighter than gasoline and require less support.
   c. The baffles cause syrups to congeal.

8. The amount that a liquid can expand in transit can be affected by?
   a. The grade that is being pulled
   b. The suddenness with which the brakes are applied
   c. The temperature of the load

9. What is a reason for filling a tank only partially?
   a. The shipper ordered a small quantity.
   b. The shipment was too light in weight.
   c. The tank had a hole that leaked liquid.

10. Why is the stopping of a tank vehicle on a slippery surface extra hazardous?
    a. Liquid surge will tend to shove the vehicle ahead.
    b. A vehicle on a slippery surface can become stuck more easily.
    c. The wave of the liquid inside the tank may hit the rear of the tank.

Part Three

1. What is overturn protection?
   a. Guards to protect fittings and valves in case of a rollover
   b. Weight reducers that will cause the trailer to ride lower
   c. Guards that keep a tractor from turning too sharply and breaking air lines

2. When you load a tank that has bulkheads, it is most important to check?
   a. The size of the hose connections
   b. The size of the bulkheads
   c. Weight distribution of the commodity being loaded

3. What is a dome cover?
   a. A cover to protect an opening where a tank is filled
   b. A cover to protect a drain on the bottom of the tank
   c. An extra cover to protect the cab in case of a rollover

4. If transporting flammable cargo over a railroad track you may shift gears?
   a. When the sound of your engine tells you it is time to shift gears
   b. When your tachometer shows 1100 RPM or higher
   c. Do not shift gears when crossing over railroad tracks.

5. How soon can you remove placards when you unload flammables from a tanker?
   a. After you have completed unloading, but before you drive away
   b. Before you start to unload or during the unloading
   c. After the tank has been cleaned or another commodity has been loaded

6. What can liquid surge do to the handling of a tank vehicle?
   a. Surge improves your ability to turn corners tighter.
   b. Surge may move the vehicle in the direction the liquid moves in the tank.
   c. Surge causes tank contamination.

7. A vehicle with empty tanks may?
   a. Be stopped more quickly with the emergency brakes
   b. Require a greater stopping distance than a loaded tanker
   c. Have better traction at all times than does a loaded tanker

8. Which is true about the emergency steering of tankers?
   a. Do not apply the brakes when making a quick turn.
   b. Countersteering is easy with a loaded tanker.
   c. Never try to stop a tanker without turning.

9. When loading a tanker you must consider weight distribution because?
   a. You do not want to put too much weight on the front or on the rear.
   b. Computers will not check this for you.
   c. Tanks cannot be bent or strained.

10. A 'tank vehicle' includes any portable tank having a liquid capacity of?
    a. 100 gallons or more
    b. 500 gallons or more
    c. 1,000 gallons or more

Answer Key

Part One

1. C: Transit mix trucks and cement mixers
2. C: Space that must be left in a cargo tank for liquids to expand
3. A: Different liquids expand by different amounts.
4. A: A high center of gravity and the liquid surge of the cargo transported
5. B: A liquid-tight division of a tank
6. B: Bulkheads are liquid-tight and baffles have holes in them.
7. C: The weight of the liquid.
8. A: The legal weight and load limits of your vehicle
9. B: The amount that the liquid might expand in transit
10. A: Liquid has more room to move in a partially-filled tank.

Part Two

1. C: Roll over
2. C: Not necessarily
3. B: Yes, forward and back surge is strong in smooth bore tankers.
4. C: Side-to-side surge
5. C: It will tend to move the vehicle in the direction that the liquid moves.
6. A: Will have less front-to-back surge
7. A: Sanitation regulations often forbid the use of baffles.
8. C: The temperature of the load
9. A: The shipper ordered a small quantity.
10. A: Liquid surge will tend to shove the vehicle ahead.

Part Three

1. A: Guards to protect fittings and valves in case of a rollover
2. C: Weight distribution of the commodity being loaded
3. A: A cover to protect an opening where a tank is filled
4. C: Do not shift gears when crossing over railroad tracks.
5. C: After the tank has been cleaned or another commodity has been loaded
6. B: Surge may move the vehicle in the direction the liquid moves in the tank.
7. B: Require a greater stopping distance than a loaded tanker
8. A: Do not apply the brakes when making a quick turn.
9. A: You do not want to put too much weight on the front or on the rear.
10. C: 1,000 gallons or more

Combination Vehicles (Doubles and Triples) Endorsement

Trailer hand valve

The trailer hand valve (also called the trolley valve or Johnson bar) works the trailer brakes. The trailer hand valve should be used only to test the trailer brakes. Do not use it in driving because of the danger of making the trailer skid. The foot brake sends air to all of the brakes on the vehicle (including the trailer(s)). There is much less danger of causing a skid or jackknife when using just the foot brake. Never use the hand valve for parking because all the air might leak out unlocking the brakes (in trailers that don't have spring brakes). Always use the parking brakes when parking. If the trailer does not have spring brakes, use wheel chocks to keep the trailer from moving.

Tractor protection valve

The tractor protection valve keeps air in the tractor or truck brake system should the trailer break away or develop a bad leak. The tractor protection valve is controlled by the "trailer air supply" control valve in the cab. The control valve allows you to open and shut the tractor protection valve. The tractor protection valve will close automatically if air pressure is low (in the range of 20 to 45 psi). When the tractor protection valve closes, it stops any air from going out of the tractor. It also lets the air out of the trailer emergency line. This causes the trailer emergency brakes to come on, with possible loss of control. (Emergency brakes are covered later.)

Trailer air supply control

The trailer air supply control on newer vehicles is a red eight-sided knob, which you use to control the tractor protection valve. You push it in to supply the trailer with air, and pull it out to shut the air off and put on the trailer emergency brakes. The valve will pop out (thus closing the tractor protection valve) when the air pressure drops into the range of 20 to 45 psi. Tractor protection valve controls or "emergency" valves on older vehicles may not operate automatically. There may be a lever rather than a knob. The "normal" position is used for pulling a trailer. The "emergency" position is used to shut the air off and put on the trailer emergency brakes.

Trailer air lines

Every combination vehicle has two air lines, the service line and the emergency line. They run between each vehicle (tractor to trailer, trailer to dolly, dolly to second trailer, etc.)

Service air line
The service line (also called the control line or signal line) carries air, which is controlled by the foot brake or the trailer hand brake. Depending on how hard you press the foot brake or hand valve, the pressure in the service line will similarly change. The service line is connected to relay valves. These valves allow the trailer brakes to be applied more quickly than would otherwise be possible.

Emergency air line
The emergency line (also called the supply line) has two purposes. First, it supplies air to the trailer air tanks. Second, the emergency line controls the emergency brakes on combination vehicles. Loss of air pressure in the emergency line causes the trailer emergency brakes to come on. The pressure loss could be caused by a trailer breaking loose, thus tearing apart the emergency air hose. Or it could be caused by a hose, metal tubing, or other part breaking, letting the air out. When the emergency line loses pressure, it also causes the tractor protection valve to close (the air supply knob will pop out). Emergency lines are often coded with the color red (red hose, red couplers, or other parts) to keep from getting them mixed up with the blue service line.

Hose couplers or glad hands

Glad hands are coupling devices used to connect the service and emergency air lines from the truck or tractor to the trailer. The couplers have a rubber seal, which prevents air from escaping. Clean the couplers and rubber seals before a connection is made. When connecting the glad hands, press the two seals together with the couplers at a 90 degree angle to each other. A turn of the glad hand attached to the hose will join and lock the couplers. It helps if you moisten the rubber seals. When coupling, make sure to couple the proper glad hands together. To help avoid mistakes, colors are sometimes used. Blue is used for the service lines and red for the emergency (supply) lines. Sometimes, metal tags are attached to the lines with the words "service" and "emergency" stamped on them.

If you do cross the air lines, supply air will be sent to the service line instead of going to charge the trailer air tanks. Air will not be available to release the trailer spring brakes (parking brakes). If the spring brakes don't release when you push the trailer air supply control, check the air line connections. Older trailers do not have spring brakes. If the air supply in the trailer air tank has leaked away there will be no emergency brakes, and the trailer wheels will turn freely. If you crossed the air lines, you could drive away but you wouldn't have trailer brakes. This would be very dangerous. Always test the trailer brakes before driving with the hand valve or by pulling the air supply (tractor protection valve) control. Pull gently against them in a low gear to make sure the brakes work.

Some vehicles have "dead end" or dummy couplers to which the hoses may be attached when they are not in use. This will prevent water and dirt from getting into the coupler and the air lines. Use the dummy couplers when the air lines are not connected to a trailer. If there are no dummy couplers, the glad hands can sometimes be locked together (depending on the couplings). It is very important to keep the air supply clean.

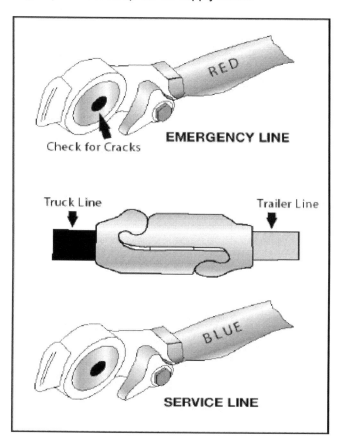

80

Trailer air tanks

Each trailer and converter dolly has one or more air tanks. They are filled by the emergency (supply) line from the tractor. They provide the air pressure used to operate trailer brakes. Air pressure is sent from the air tanks to the brakes by relay valves. The pressure in the service line tells how much pressure the relay valves should send to the trailer brakes. The pressure in the service line is controlled by the brake pedal (and the trailer hand brake). It is important that you don't let water and oil build up in the air tanks. If you do, the brakes may not work correctly. Each tank has a drain valve on it and you should drain each tank every day. If your tanks have automatic drains, they will keep most moisture out. But you should still open the drains to make sure.

Shut-off valves

Shut-off valves (also called cut-out cocks) are used in the service and supply air lines at the back of trailers used to tow other trailers. These valves permit closing the air lines off when another trailer is not being towed. You must check that all shut-off valves are in the open position except the ones at the back of the last trailer, which must be closed.

Trailer service, parking and emergency brakes

New trailers have spring brakes just like trucks and truck tractors. Converter dollies and trailers built before 1975 are not required to have spring brakes. Trailers that do not have spring brakes have emergency brakes which work from the air stored in the trailer air tank. The emergency brakes come on whenever air pressure in the emergency line is lost. These trailers do not have a parking brake. The emergency brakes come on whenever the air supply knob is pulled out or the trailer is disconnected. But, the brakes will not hold if there is not sufficient air pressure in the trailer air tank. Eventually, the air will leak away and there will be no brake. Therefore, always use wheel chocks when you park trailers without spring brakes. A major leak in the emergency line will cause the tractor protection valve to close and the trailer emergency brakes to come on. You may not notice a leak in the service line until you put the brakes on. Then, the air loss from the leak will lower the air tank pressure quickly. If it goes low enough, the trailer emergency brakes will come on.

Inspecting Combination Vehicles

Coupling system and landing gear

Check the fifth wheel (lower):
- Securely mounted to frame.
- No missing or damaged parts.
- Make sure there is enough grease (if the trailer is not hooked up).
- No visible space between the upper and lower fifth wheel.
- Locking jaws around the shank, **not** the head of the kingpin.
- Release arm properly seated and safety latch/lock engaged.

Check the fifth wheel (upper):
- Glide plate securely mounted to trailer frame.
- Kingpin not damaged.

Check the sliding fifth wheel:
- Slide not damaged or parts missing.
- Properly greased.
- All locking pins present and locked in place.
- If air powered--no air leaks.
- Check that fifth wheel is not so far forward that the tractor frame will hit the landing gear, or the cab will hit the trailer, during turns.

Check the air and electric lines to the trailer:
- Electrical cord firmly plugged in and secured.
- Air lines properly connected to glad hands, no air leaks, properly secured with enough slack for turns.
- All lines free from damage.

Check the landing gear:
- Fully raised, no missing parts, not bent or otherwise damaged.
- Crank handle in place and secured.
- If power operated, no air or hydraulic leaks.

Doubles and triples

Inspect the double and triple trailers:
- Shut-off valves (at rear of trailers, in service and emergency lines):
  - Rear of front trailers: OPEN.
  - Rear of last trailer: CLOSED.
  - Converter dolly air tank drain valve: CLOSED.
- Be sure air lines are supported and glad hands are properly connected.
- If spare tire is carried on converter gear (dolly), make sure it's secured.
- Be sure pintle-eye of dolly is in place in pintle hook of trailer(s).
- Make sure pintle hook is latched.
- Safety chains should be secured to trailer(s).
- Be sure light cords are firmly in sockets on trailers.

Air brakes

Make these checks in addition to the pre-trip checks that you make for your air brakes. The following section explains how to check air brakes on combination vehicles. Check the airbrakes on a double or triple trailer the same way you check them for any combination vehicle.

- Check that air flows to all trailers:
    - Use the tractor parking brake and/or chock the wheels to hold the vehicle.
    - Wait for air pressure to reach normal, then push in the red "trailer air supply" knob. This will supply air to the emergency (supply) lines.
    - Use the trailer handbrake to provide air to the service line.
    - Go to the rear of the rig. Open the emergency line shut-off valve at the rear of the last trailer. You should hear air escaping, showing the entire system is charged.
    - Close the emergency line valve.
    - Open the service line valve to check that service pressure goes through all the trailers (this test assumes that the trailer handbrake or the service brake pedal is on), and then close the valve. If you do NOT hear air escaping from both lines, check that the shut-off valves on the trailers and dollies are in the OPEN position. You MUST have air all the way to the back for all the brakes to work.
- Test tractor protection valve:
    - Charge the trailer air brake system. (That is, build up normal air pressure and push the "air supply" knob in.)
    - Shut the engine off.
    - Step on and off the brake pedal several times to reduce the air pressure in the tanks.
    - The trailer air supply control (also called the tractor protection valve control) should pop out (or go from "normal" to "emergency" position) when the air pressure falls into the pressure range specified by the manufacturer. (Usually within the range of 20 to 45 psi.)
    - If the tractor protection valve doesn't work right, an air hose or trailer brake leak could drain all the air from the tractor. This would cause the emergency brakes to come on, with possible loss of control.
- Test the trailer emergency brakes:
    - Charge the trailer air brake system and check that the trailer rolls freely.
    - Then stop and pull out the trailer air supply control (also called tractor protection valve control or trailer emergency valve) or place it in the "emergency" position.
    - Pull gently on the trailer with the tractor to check that the trailer emergency brakes are on.
- Test the trailer service brakes:
    - Check for normal air pressure, release the parking brakes, move the vehicle forward slowly, and apply trailer brakes with the hand control (trolley valve), if so equipped. You should feel the brakes come on.
    This tells you the trailer brakes are connected and working. (The trailer brakes should be tested with the hand valve but controlled in normal operation with the foot pedal, which applies air to the service brakes at all wheels.)

Note: The trailer brakes should be tested with the hand valve. In normal operation, however, control the trailer brakes with the foot pedal. The foot pedal applies air to the service brakes at all wheels.

Coupling and Uncoupling Combination Vehicles

Coupling and uncoupling

Coupling and uncoupling is basic to the safe operation of combination vehicles. Wrong coupling and uncoupling can be dangerous. The makes and models of rigs are different. So, learn the details of coupling and uncoupling for the trucks that you will operate.

Coupling tractor-semitrailers

Inspect the fifth wheel:
- Check for damaged/missing parts.
- Check to see that mounting to the tractor is secure. Make sure there are no cracks in the frame.
- Be sure that the fifth wheel plate is greased. Failure to keep the fifth wheel plate greased could cause steering problems because of friction between the tractor and trailer.
- Check if fifth wheel is in the proper position for coupling:
  - The wheel should be tilted down toward the rear of the tractor.
  - The jaws should be open.
  - The safety unlocking handle should be in the automatic lock position.
- If you have a sliding fifth wheel, make sure it is locked.
- Make sure that the trailer kingpin is not bent or broken.

Inspect the area and chock the wheels:
- Make sure the area around the vehicle is clear.
- Be sure the trailer wheels are chocked or the spring brakes are on.
- Be sure that cargo is secured so that it will not move while the tractor is being coupled to the trailer.

Position tractor:
- Put the tractor directly in front of the trailer. Never back under the trailer at an angle. This could cause the trailer to move sideways and break the landing gear.
- Check position, using outside mirrors, by looking down both sides of the trailer.

Back slowly:
- Back until the fifth wheel just touches the trailer.
- Don't hit the trailer.

Secure tractor:
- Put on the parking brake.
- Put the transmission in neutral.

Check trailer height:
- The trailer should be low enough that it is raised slightly by the tractor when the tractor is backed under it. Raise or lower the trailer as needed. (If the trailer is too low, the tractor may strike and damage the trailer nose; if the trailer is too high, it may not couple correctly.)
- Check that the kingpin and fifth wheel are aligned.

Connect the air lines to the trailer:
- Check the glad hand seals and connect the tractor emergency air line to the trailer emergency glad hand.
- Check the glad hand seals and connect the tractor service air line to the trailer service glad hand.
- Make sure the air lines are safely supported so that they won't be crushed or caught while you back the tractor under the trailer.

Supply air to the trailer:
- From cab, push in "air supply" knob or move tractor protection valve control from the "emergency" to the "normal" position to supply air to the trailer brake system.
- Wait until the air pressure is normal.
- Check brake system for crossed air lines.
  - Shut engine off so you can hear the brakes.
  - Apply and release trailer brakes and listen for sound of trailer brakes being applied and released. You should hear the brakes move when applied and air escape when the brakes are released.
  - Check air brake system pressure gauge for signs of major air loss.
- When you are sure trailer brakes are working, start engine.
- Make sure the air pressure is up to normal.

Lock the trailer brakes:
- Pull out the trailer air supply knob or move the tractor protection valve from normal to emergency.

Back under the trailer:
- Use the lowest reverse gear.
- Back the tractor slowly under the trailer to avoid hitting the kingpin too hard.
- Stop when the kingpin is locked into the fifth wheel.

Check the connection for security:
- Raise the trailer landing gear slightly off the ground.
- Pull the tractor gently forward while the trailer brakes are locked to be sure that the trailer is locked onto the tractor.
- Secure the vehicle.
- Put the transmission in neutral.
- Put on the parking brakes.
- Shut off the engine. Take the key with you so someone else won't move the truck while you are under it.

Inspect the coupling:
- Use a flashlight if necessary.
- Make sure that there is no space between the upper and lower fifth wheel. If there is space, something is wrong. The kingpin may be on top of closed fifth wheel jaws and the trailer would come loose very easily.
- Go under the trailer and look into the back of the fifth wheel. Make sure the fifth wheel jaws have closed around the shank of the kingpin. Refer to the diagram:

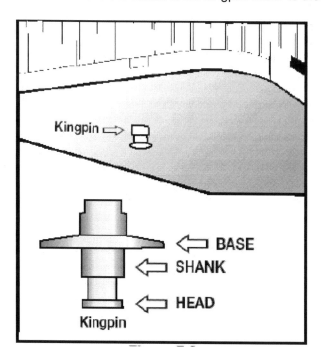

- Check that the locking lever is in the lock position.
- Check that the safety latch is in the position over the locking lever. On some fifth wheels the catch must be put in place by hand.
- If the coupling isn't right, don't drive the coupled unit. Get it fixed.

Connect the electrical cord and check the air lines:
- Plug the electrical cord into the trailer and fasten the safety catch.
- Check the air lines and electrical lines for signs of damage.
- Make sure the air and electrical lines will not hit any moving parts of the vehicle.

Raise the front trailer supports (landing gear):
- Use low gear range to begin raising the landing gear. Once free of weight, switch to the high gear range.
- Raise the landing gear all the way up. Never drive with the landing gear part of the way up. It could catch on railroad tracks or other things.
- After raising the landing gear, secure the crank handle.
- When the full weight of the trailer is resting on the tractor:
- Check for enough clearance between the rear of the tractor frame and the landing gear. When the tractor turns sharply, it must not hit the landing gear.
- Check that there is enough clearance between the top of the tractor tires and the nose of the trailer.

Remove the trailer wheel chocks and store in a safe place.

Uncoupling tractor-semitrailers

Position the rig:
- Make sure the surface of the parking area can support the weight of the trailer.
- Line up the tractor with the trailer. Pulling out at an angle can damage the landing gear.

Ease the pressure on the locking jaws:
- Shut off the trailer air supply to lock the trailer brakes.
- Ease pressure on the fifth wheel locking jaws by backing up gently. This will help you release the fifth wheel locking lever.
- Put the parking brakes on while the tractor is pushing against the kingpin. This will hold the rig with pressure off the locking jaws.

Chock the trailer wheels:
- Chock the trailer wheels if the trailer doesn't have spring brakes or if you aren't sure. The air could leak out of the trailer air tank and release the emergency brakes. Without chocks, the trailer could move.

Lower the landing gear:
- If the trailer is empty, lower the landing gear until it makes firm contact with the ground.
- If the trailer is loaded, turn the crank in low gear a few extra turns after the landing gear makes firm contact with the ground. This will lift some weight off the tractor. This makes it easier to unlatch the fifth wheel. It also makes it easier to couple next time.

Disconnect the air lines and electrical cable:
- Disconnect the air lines from the trailer. Connect the glad hands to the dummy couplers at the back of the cab or couple them together.
- Hang the electrical cable with the plug down to prevent moisture from entering it.
- Make sure the lines are supported so they won't be damaged while driving the tractor.

Unlock the fifth wheel:
- Raise the release handle lock.
- Pull the release handle to the open position.
- Keep your feet and legs clear of the rear tractor wheels to avoid serious injury in case the vehicle moves.

Pull the tractor partly clear of the trailer:
- Pull the tractor forward until the fifth wheel comes out from under the trailer.
- Stop with the tractor frame under the trailer. This prevents the trailer from falling to the ground if the landing gear collapses or sinks.

Secure the tractor:
- Apply the parking brake.
- Place the transmission in neutral.

Inspect the trailer supports:
- Make sure the ground is supporting the trailer.
- Make sure the landing gear is not damaged.

Pull the tractor clear of the trailer.
- Release the parking brakes.
- Check the area and drive the tractor forward until it clears the trailer.

Coupling twin trailers

Secure the second (rear) trailer:
- If the second trailer doesn't have spring brakes, drive the tractor close to the trailer.
- Connect the emergency line and charge the trailer air tank.
- Disconnect the emergency line.
- If the slack adjusters are set correctly, this will set the trailer emergency brakes.
- If you aren't sure about the trailer brakes, chock the wheels.

Couple the tractor and first semi-trailer.
- To couple the tractor and first semi-trailer, follow the steps in Section 3: Combination Vehicles.

Position the converter dolly in front of the second (rear) trailer:
- Release the dolly brakes by opening the dolly air tank petcock. If the dolly has spring brakes, use the dolly parking brake control.
- If it isn't too far, wheel the dolly into position by hand. Line it up with the kingpin.
- Or, use the tractor and first semi-trailer to pick up the converter dolly.
  - Position the combination (tractor and first semi-trailer) as close as possible to the converter dolly.
  - Move the dolly to the rear of the first semi-trailer and couple it to the trailer.
  - Lock the pintle hook.
  - Secure the dolly support in the raised position.
  - Pull the dolly into position as close as possible to the nose of the second semi-trailer.
  - Lower the dolly support.
  - Unhook the dolly from the first trailer.
  - Wheel the dolly into position in front of the second trailer in line with the kingpin.

Connect the converter dolly to the front trailer:
- Back the first semi-trailer into position in front of the dolly tongue.
- Hook the dolly to the front trailer.
  - Lock the pintle hook.
  - Secure the converter gear support in the raised position.
- Be sure that the trailer brakes are locked or that the wheels are chocked.
- Make sure the trailer height is correct. It must be slightly lower than the center of the fifth wheel so that the trailer is raised slightly when the dolly is pushed under it.
- Back the converter dolly under the rear trailer.
- Raise the landing gear slightly off the ground to prevent damage if the trailer moves.
- Test the coupling by pulling against the pin of the rear semi-trailer.
- Make a visual check of the coupling.
  - Make sure that there is no space between the upper and lower fifth wheel. If there is, something is wrong.
  - Make sure the fifth wheel jaws have closed around the shank of the kingpin.
- Connect the safety chains, air hoses and light cords.
- Close the converter dolly air tank petcock and shut-off valves at the rear of the second trailer. The service and emergency line shut-off valve at the rear of the second trailer should be closed.
- Open the shut-off valves at the rear of the first trailer and on the dolly.
- Raise the landing gear.
- Charge the trailers' air supply.
  - Push in the trailer air supply knob.
  - Check for air at the rear of the second trailer by opening the emergency line shut-off valve.
  - If there is no air pressure there, something is wrong and the brakes won't work.

Uncoupling twin trailers

Uncoupling the rear trailer:
- Park the rig in a straight line on firm level ground.
- Apply the parking brakes so that the rig won't move.
- Chock the wheels on the second trailer if it doesn't have spring brakes.
- Lower the landing gear of the second trailer enough to remove some weight from the dolly.
- Close the air shut-off valve at the rear of the first trailer and on the dolly.
- Disconnect all dolly air and electric lines and secure them.
- Release the dolly brakes.
- Release the converter dolly fifth wheel latch.
- Slowly pull the tractor, first trailer and dolly forward to pull the dolly from under the second trailer.

Uncouple the converter dolly:
- Lower the dolly landing gear.
- Disconnect the safety chains.
- Apply the converter gear spring brakes or chock the wheels.
- Release the pintle hook on the first trailer.
- Slowly pull clear of the dolly.

  Caution: Never unlock the pintle hook with the dolly still under the rear trailer. The dolly tow bar could fly up. This could cause injury and would make it very difficult to re-couple.

Coupling and uncoupling triple trailers

Couple the second and third trailers:
- Couple second and third trailers using the method of coupling doubles.
- Uncouple the tractor and pull away from the second and third trailers.

Couple the tractor and first trailer to the second and third trailers:
- Couple the tractor to the first trailer. Move the converter dolly into position and couple the first trailer to the second trailer using the steps outlined for coupling doubles. The triple rig is now complete.

Uncouple the triple rig:
- Uncouple the third trailer by pulling out the dolly. Then unhitch the dolly using the steps outlined for uncoupling doubles.
- Uncouple the rest of the rig the same way you would uncouple a double-bottom rig. Follow the steps already outlined.

Driving Combination Vehicles

Rollovers

More than half of truck driver deaths in crashes are the result of truck rollovers. When more cargo is piled up in a truck, the "center of gravity" moves higher up from the road. The truck becomes easier to turn over. Fully loaded rigs are ten times more likely to roll over in a crash than empty rigs. The following two things will help you prevent rollover:

- Keep the cargo as close to the ground as possible, and drive slowly around turns. Keeping cargo low is even more important in combination vehicles than in straight trucks. Also, keep the load centered on your rig. If the load is to one side so it makes a trailer lean, a rollover is more likely. Make sure your cargo is centered and spread out as much as possible.
- Rollovers happen when you turn too fast. Drive slowly around corners, on ramps, and off ramps. Avoid quick lane changes, especially when fully loaded.

Rearward amplification and the crack-the-whip effect

"Rearward amplification" causes the crack-the-whip effect. See the chart below for the eight types of combination vehicles and the rearward amplification each has in a quick lane change. Rigs with the least crack-the-whip effect are shown at the top and those with the most, at the bottom. Rearward amplification of 2.0 in the chart means that the rear trailer is twice as likely to turn over as the tractor. You can see that triples have a rearward amplification of 3.5. This means you can roll the last trailer of triples 3.5 times as easily as a five-axle tractor.

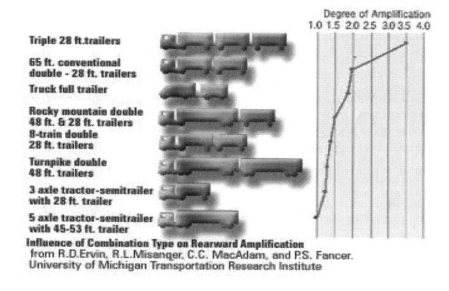

Influence of Combination Type on Rearward Amplification
from R.D.Ervin, R.L.Misanger, C.C. MacAdam, and P.S. Fancer.
University of Michigan Transportation Research Institute

Steering

Steer gently and smoothly when you are pulling trailers. If you make a sudden movement with your steering wheel, your trailer could tip over. Follow far enough behind other vehicles (at least 1 second for each 10 feet of your vehicle length, plus another second if going over 40 mph). Look far enough down the road to avoid being surprised and having to make a sudden lane change. At night, drive slowly enough to see obstacles with your headlights before it is too late to change lanes or stop gently. Slow down to a safe speed before going into a turn.

Braking

Control your speed whether fully loaded or empty. Large combination vehicles take longer to stop when they are empty than when they are fully loaded. When lightly loaded, the very stiff suspension springs and strong brakes give poor traction and make it very easy to lock up the wheels. Your trailer can swing out and strike other vehicles. Your tractor can jackknife very quickly. You also must be very careful about driving "bobtail" tractors (tractors without semitrailers). Tests have shown that bobtails can be very hard to stop smoothly. It takes them longer to stop than a tractor-semitrailer loaded to maximum gross weight. In any combination rig, allow lots of following distance and look far ahead, so you can brake early. Don't be caught by surprise and have to make a "panic" stop.

Railroad-highway crossings

Railroad-highway crossings can also cause problems, particularly when pulling trailers with low underneath clearance. These trailers can get stuck on raised crossings:
- Low slung units (lowboy, car carrier, moving van, possum-belly livestock trailer).
- Single-axle tractor pulling a long trailer with its landing gear set to accommodate a tandem-axle tractor.

If for any reason you get stuck on the tracks, get out of the vehicle and away from the tracks. Check signposts or signal housing at the crossing for emergency notification information. Call 911 or other emergency number. Give the location of the crossing using all identifiable landmarks, especially the DOT number, if posted.

Preventing skids

When the wheels of a trailer lock up, the trailer will tend to swing around. This is more likely to happen when the trailer is empty or lightly loaded. This type of jackknife is often called a "trailer jackknife." The procedure for stopping a trailer skid is:
- Recognize the skid. The earliest and best way to recognize that the trailer has started to skid is by seeing it in your mirrors. Any time you apply the brakes hard, check the mirrors to make sure the trailer is staying where it should be. Once the trailer swings out of your lane, it's very difficult to prevent a jackknife.
- Stop using the brake. Release the brakes to get traction back. Do not use the trailer hand brake (if you have one) to "straighten out the rig." This is the wrong thing to do since the brakes on the trailer wheels caused the skid in the first place. Once the trailer wheels grip the road again, the trailer will start to follow the tractor and straighten out.

91

Offtracking

When a vehicle goes around a corner, the rear wheels follow a different path than the front wheels. This is called "offtracking" or "cheating." The figure below shows how offtracking causes the path followed by a tractor to be wider than the rig itself. Longer vehicles will offtrack more. The rear wheels of the powered unit (truck or tractor) will offtrack some, and the rear wheels of the trailer will offtrack even more. If there is more than one trailer, the rear wheels of the last trailer will offtrack the most.

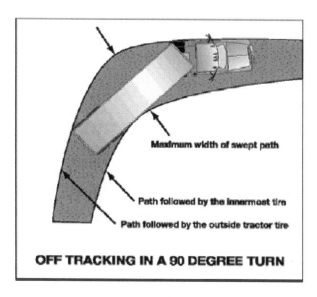

Steering

Steer the front end wide enough around a corner so the rear end does not run over the curb, pedestrians, etc. However, keep the rear of your vehicle close to the curb. This will stop other drivers from passing you on the right. If you cannot complete your turn without entering another traffic lane, turn wide as you complete the turn. This is better than swinging wide to the left before starting the turn because it will keep other drivers from passing you on the right.

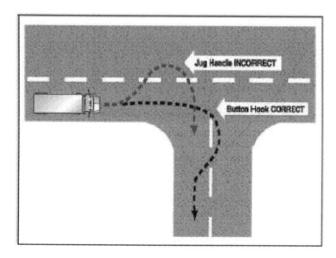

Pulling double/triple trailers

Prevent roll-overs:
- Double and triple tractor-trailer combinations are less stable than other commercial vehicles. Therefore, steer gently and go slowly around curves, corners and on-and off ramps.
- Remember, a safe speed on a curve for a straight truck or a single trailer combination vehicle may be too fast for a set of double or triple trailers.

Beware of the crack-the-whip effect:
- Doubles and triples are more likely to turn over than other combination vehicles because of the crack the-whip effect. You must steer gently when pulling trailers. The last trailer in a combination is the most likely one to turn over.

Look ahead:
- You must drive doubles and triples very smoothly to prevent a rollover or jackknife. Therefore, look far ahead so you can slow down or change lanes gradually if necessary.

Manage your space:
- Doubles and triples take up more space than other commercial vehicles. They are longer and also need more space because you cannot turn or stop them suddenly.
- Allow more following distance.
- Make sure you have large enough gaps before entering or crossing traffic.
- Be sure you are clear on the side before you change lanes.

Be even more careful in adverse conditions:
- In bad weather, slippery conditions or when driving in the mountains, you must be very careful when driving doubles and triples.

Combination Vehicles Endorsement Tests

Part One

1. What is the cause of more than half the truck driver deaths in crashes?
    a. Rush hour traffic.
    b. Truck rollovers.
    c. Heart attacks.

2. Are fully loaded rigs more likely to roll over in a crash than empty rigs?
    a. There is no difference as to the load so far as rolling over is concerned.
    b. Fully loaded rigs are less likely to roll over in a crash.
    c. Fully loaded rigs are 10 times more likely to roll over in a crash.

3. What two things can a driver do to prevent rollovers?
    a. Keep the cargo as close to the ground as possible. Go slowly around turns.
    b. Go slowly around turns. Try to raise the center of gravity of your load.
    c. Accelerate slowly. Slow down quickly.

4. When you make a quick lane change, the trailer only may overturn. What is the effect called that produces this result?
    a. The crack-the-whip effect.
    b. The worm effect.
    c. The hula effect.

5. Since a sudden movement with your steering wheel can tip a trailer over, how far behind other vehicles should you follow when pulling trailers.
    a. At least one second for each unit of your vehicle plus another second if going over 45 miles per hour.
    b. At least one second for each 20 feet of your vehicle length, plus another second if going over 35 miles per hour.
    c. At least one second for each ten feet of your vehicle length, plus another second if going over 40 miles per hour.

6. What are some things that you can do to avoid getting surprised and having to make a sudden lane change?
    a. Use your highbeam headlights at all times. Look far ahead all the time.
    b. Slow down to a safe speed before going into a turn. Focus your attention on the taillights of the vehicle ahead.
    c. Look far enough down the road and allow lots of following distance.

7. Why do large combination vehicles that are empty take longer to stop than when they are fully loaded?
    a. When lightly loaded, stiff suspension springs and strong brakes give poor traction and make it easy to lock up the wheels.
    b. Combination vehicles are longer than bobtails and therefore require more length to stop.
    c. Empty trucks are harder to control and the brake connections are more likely to come loose.

8. Why must you be extra careful when bobtailing?
    a. Bobtails may not be equipped with splash guards or back bumpers.
    b. Bobtails stop more smoothly but take longer to stop.
    c. Bobtails can be hard to stop smoothly and take longer to stop than a loaded tractor-semi trailer.

9. When the wheels of a trailer lock up, what will the trailer tend to do?
   a. The trailer will immediately stop.
   b. The trailer will tend to jackknife or swing around.
   c. The trailer will automatically break loose from the fifth wheel assembly.

10. Why should you check your mirrors whenever you apply the brakes hard?
    a. This is the best way to recognize if the trailer has started to skid.
    b. To tell if the mirrors are still in adjustment.
    c. To tell if your cargo door comes open.

Part Two

1. If your trailer has started to skid, what should you do to get traction back?
    a. Release the brakes. Don't use the trailer handbrake.
    b. Press harder on the brake pedal to stop the vehicle faster.
    c. Set the trailer handbrake.

2. What is it called when the rear wheels follow a different path than the front wheels when a vehicle goes around a corner?
    a. A close fit.
    b. Offtracking.
    c. Crack-the-whip effect.

3. What are two reasons why doubles and triples take up more space than other commercial vehicles?
    a. They are longer and they cannot be turned or stopped suddenly.
    b. They are longer and weave from side to side.
    c. They are longer and are taller than tractors.

4. In allowing more space, what should you do before entering or crossing traffic?
    a. Move quickly because you have a deadline.
    b. Because of the large size of your vehicle expect others to see you and make room for you.
    c. Make sure there are large enough gaps before entering or crossing traffic.

5. What is a reason why there is more chance of skids with doubles and triples in bad weather, slippery conditions and mountain driving?
    a. Your drive wheels provide security for the pulling unit only.
    b. Your front wheels may not be equipped with brakes.
    c. You have more length and more dead axles to pull.

6. When can you use the trailer hand valve for parking a combination vehicle?
    a. Always.
    b. When the emergency brake is not working.
    c. Never.

7. In normal driving should you ever use the trailer hand valve before the brake pedal to prevent trailer skids?
    a. Always
    b. When the brake pedal does not work.
    c. Never.

8. Which valve keeps air in the tractor or truck if the trailer breaks away or develops a bad leak?
    a. The one-way check valve.
    b. The relay valve.
    c. The tractor protection valve.

9. If the tractor protection valve closes, letting air out of the trailer emergency line, which brakes should come on?
    a. The trailer handbrake.
    b. The trailer emergency brakes.
    c. The brakes on the front axle.

10. What happens when you push in the trailer air supply control knob and what happens when you pull it out?

    a. Push it in to supply the trailer with air. Pull it out to release all air to the trailer.

    b. Pull it out to release all air to the trailer. Do not push it in when the vehicle is underway.

    c. Push it in to supply the trailer with air. Pull it out to shut the air off and put on the trailer emergency brakes.

Part Three

1. On older vehicles there may be a lever, rather than a knob, for the tractor protection valve. What are the normal and emergency positions?
    a. The normal position is used for pulling a trailer. The emergency position is used to shut air off to the trailer.
    b. The normal position is horizontal. The emergency position is vertical.
    c. The normal position is used for supplying air to the drive wheel brakes. The emergency position is used to substitute for the emergency brakes.

2. Which valves on the service line on the trailer connect the trailer air tanks to the trailer air brakes?
    a. One-way check valves.
    b. Relay valves.
    c. Automatic valves.

3. What is one purpose of the emergency air line?
    a. It allows you to continue your trip when the primary system is malfunctioning.
    b. It activates an emergency locator transmitter.
    c. It supplies air to the trailer air tanks.

4. What happens to the trailer emergency brakes if there is a loss of pressure in the emergency line?
    a. The emergency trailer brakes will fail.
    b. The emergency trailer brakes will fade.
    c. The emergency trailer brakes will come on.

5. When the emergency line loses pressure, what happens to the tractor protection value?
    a. The valve will open.
    b. The valve will close.
    c. The valve will pop out.

6. If the air lines on a truck are color coded, which lines are blue?
    a. The emergency lines.
    b. The spring line.
    c. The service line.

7. To connect the glad hands, the tow seals are pressed together with the couplers at what kind of angle to each other?
    a. A 45 degree angle.
    b. A 90 degree angle.
    c. A 180 degree angle.

8. Why should you lock the glad hands to each other when you are not towing any trailers?
    a. To prevent brake fade.
    b. To keep the brakes from overheating.
    c. To keep dirt and water out the lines.

9. If the spring brakes do not release when you push the trailer air supply control, what should you do?
    a. Unhook the air line connections.
    b. Check the air line connections.
    c. Tighten the air line connections.

10. Do trailers made before 1975 have spring brakes?
    a. Most of them do.
    b. All of them do.
    c. Many do not.

Part Four

1. Before driving away, how can you always test the trailer brakes?
   a. With the hand valve or by pulling the tractor protection valve and then pulling against the brakes in a low gear.
   b. With the hand valve or by pulling the tractor protection valve, and accelerating.
   c. With the hand valve or by pulling the tractor protection valve, and pulling against the brakes gently at a maximum speed.

2. How are the air tanks on trailers and converter dollies filled?
   a. By the tractor protection valve.
   b. By the air compressor cut off valve.
   c. By the emergency supply line from the tractor.

3. What tells how much pressure the relay valves should send to the trailer brakes?
   a. The position of the foot pedal.
   b. The position of the brake linings.
   c. The pressure in the service line.

4. In what position should the air line shut off valves be when you check them?
   a. They should be in the open position except at the back of the last trailer.
   b. They should be in the open position.
   c. They should be in the closed position.

5. What should you use to be safe when you park trailers that don't have spring brakes?
   a. Use wheel chocks
   b. Use available rocks.
   c. Use the curb.

6. What happens if (only) the service line comes apart while you are driving?
   a. You may not notice anything until you try to put the brakes on when air loss from the leak will quickly lower the air tank pressure.
   b. Nothing will happen.
   c. You will hear a loud explosion.

7. Why must the fifth wheel plate have enough grease?
   a. To prevent sparks - and smoke.
   b. To prevent squealing.
   c. To prevent steering problems.

8. Before backing up how should you position the tractor in relation to the trailer?
   a. Slightly to the left of the trailer.
   b. Slightly to the left of the center of the trailer.
   c. Directly in front of the trailer.

9. Before you back under a semi-trailer in coupling your tractor at what height should the trailer be?
   a. Four feet eight inches.
   b. Well above the top of the fifth wheel.
   c. Just below the middle of the fifth wheel.

10. You have connected the air lines but have not yet backed under the trailer. What should you do?
   a. Check the light connections.
   b. Supply air to the trailer electrical system.
   c. Supply air to the trailer system.

Part Five

1. Before you back under the trailer, you should be sure that the trailer brakes are?
    a. Disengaged (Unapplied).
    b. Locked (Applied).
    c. Unhooked.

2. When a tractor and a trailer are coupled, how much space should there be between the upper and lower fifth wheel.
    a. No space.
    b. Space enough to allow air to flow freely.
    c. Seven eight's inch.

3. After you lock the kingpin into the fifth wheel how can you check the connection?
    a. By tapping it with a rubber hammer.
    b. By pulling the tractor ahead gently with the trailer brakes locked.
    c. By pulling it by hand.

4. Looking into the back of the fifth wheel, which part of the kingpin should the locking jaws close around?
    a. The skid plate.
    b. The pickup ramp.
    c. The shank of the kingpin.

5. For the coupling to be complete for a fifth wheel with a locking lever, where must the safety catch for the fifth wheel locking lever be?
    a. Over the locking lever.
    b. Level with the locking lever.
    c. Under the locking lever.

6. After you have coupled the tractor with a trailer where should the landing gear be before driving away?
    a. Raised at least six inches above the ground.
    b. Raised at least one foot above the ground with the crank handle secured in its bracket.
    c. Fully raised with the crank handle secured in its bracket.

7. Inspect the coupling. You must make certain that there is enough clearance between which two of the following?
    a. Between the fifth wheel and the floor of the trailer.
    b. Between the tractor taillights and the landing gear.
    c. Between the tops of the tractor tires and the nose of the trailer.

8. If you will be pulling doubles where one trailer is more heavily loaded than the other, where should the heavier loaded trailer be placed?
    a. It should always be behind the lighter trailer.
    b. It should always be in front of the lighter trailer
    c. It should be placed where it will have the least wind resistance.

9. What should the trailer height be before you connect a converter dolly to a second or third trailer?
    a. Five feet eight inches.
    b. It must be slightly lower than the center of the fifth wheel.
    c. Four feet eight inches.

10. Why should you never unlock the pintle hook with the dolly still under the rear trailer?
   a. The dolly tow bar may fly up.
   b. There may not be enough grease on the pintle hook to enable it to ride smoothly.
   c. It may be too hard to unlock it next time.

Answer Key

Part One

1. B: Truck rollovers.
2. C: Fully loaded rigs are 10 times more likely to roll over in a crash.
3. A: Keep the cargo as close to the ground as possible. Go slowly around turns.
4. A: The crack-the-whip effect.
5. C: At least one second for each ten feet of your vehicle length, plus another second if going over 40 miles per hour.
6. C: Look far enough down the road and allow lots of following distance.
7. A: When lightly loaded, stiff suspension springs and strong brakes give poor traction and make it easy to lock up the wheels.
8. C: Bobtails can be hard to stop and take longer to stop than a loaded tractor-semi trailer.
9. B: The trailer will tend to jackknife or swing around.
10. A: This is the best way to recognize if the trailer has started to skid.

Part Two

1. A: Release the brakes. Don't use the trailer handbrake.
2. B: Offtracking.
3. A: They are longer and they cannot be turned or stopped suddenly.
4. C: Make sure there are large enough gaps before entering or crossing traffic.
5. C: You have more length and more dead axles to pull.
6. C: Never.
7. C: Never.
8. C: The tractor protection valve.
9. B: The trailer emergency brakes.
10. C: Push it in to supply the trailer with air. Pull it out to shut the air off and put on the trailer emergency brakes.

Part Three

1. A: The normal position is used for pulling a trailer. The emergency position is used to shut air off to the trailer.
2. B: Relay valves.
3. C: It supplies air to the trailer air tanks.
4. C: The emergency trailer brakes will come on.
5. B: The valve will close.
6. C: The service line.
7. B: A 90 degree angle.
8. C: To keep dirt and water out the lines.
9. B: Check the air line connections.
10. C: Many do not.

Part Four

1. A: With the hand valve or by pulling the tractor protection valve and then pulling against the brakes in a low gear.
2. C: By the emergency supply line from the tractor.
3. C: The pressure in the service line.
4. A: They should be in the open position except at the back of the last trailer.
5. A: Use wheel chocks
6. A: You may not notice anything until you try to put the brakes on when air loss from the leak will quickly lower the air tank pressure.
7. C: To prevent steering problems.
8. C: Directly in front of the trailer.
9. C: Just below the middle of the fifth wheel.
10. C: Supply air to the trailer system.

Part Five

1. B: Locked (Applied).
2. A: No space.
3. B: By pulling the tractor ahead gently with the trailer brakes locked.
4. C: The shank of the kingpin.
5. A: Over the locking lever.
6. C: Fully raised with the crank handle secured in its bracket.
7. C: Between the tops of the tractor tires and the nose of the trailer.
8. B: It should always be in front of the lighter trailer
9. B: It must be slightly lower than the center of the fifth wheel.
10. A: The dolly tow bar may fly up.

Hazardous Materials Endorsement

Introduction

Compliance with Federal motor carrier safety regulations.

"...a motor carrier or other person to whom this part is applicable must comply with the rules in parts 390 through 397, inclusive, of this subchapter when he/she is transporting hazardous materials by a motor vehicle which must be marked or placarded in accordance with § 177.823 of this title."

Hazardous materials

Hazardous materials are products that pose a risk to health, safety, and property during transportation. The term often is shortened to HAZMAT, which you may see on road signs, or to HM in government regulations. Hazardous materials include explosives, various types of gas, solids, flammable and combustible liquid, and other materials. Because of the risks involved and the potential consequences these risks impose, all levels of government regulate the handling of hazardous materials. HAZMAT endorsements are not transferable from state to state. Hazardous materials are categorized into nine major hazard classes. There are also two categories for consumer products and combustible (flammable) liquids. The following chart shows the classes and categories and gives examples of materials in each one.

Class	Class Name	Example
1	Explosives	Ammunition Dynamite Fireworks
2	Gases	Propane Oxygen Helium
3	Flammable	Gasoline Alcohol Diesel Fuel Fuel Oils
4	Flammable Solids	Matches Magnesium
5	Oxidizers	Ammonium Nitrate Hydrogen Peroxide
6	Poisons	Pesticides Arsenic
7	Radioactive	Uranium Plutonium
8	Corrosives	Hydrochloric Acid Battery Acid, Formaldehyde
9	Miscellaneous Hazardous Materials	Asbestos Airbag Inflators & Modules
None	ORM-D (Other Regulated Material - Domestic	Hair Spray or Charcoal
None	Combustible Liquids	

Hazardous materials regulations

The Code of Federal Regulations gives regulations for hazardous materials. These regulations are located in title 49, parts 171-180. You will hear these regulations referred to as 49 CFR 171-180. The Hazardous Materials Table in the regulations includes a list of hazardous materials. However, this table does not show all hazardous materials. A material is considered hazardous based on its characteristics. A shipper decides if a product meets the definition of a hazardous material in the regulations. Because the federal regulations change often, be sure that your copy is up to date. You may get a copy from your local Government Printing Office bookstore and various publishers. Union or company offices often have copies for drivers to use.

Intent of federal regulations

Transporting hazardous materials can be risky. Federal regulations tell you how to contain the material and communicate the risk. They also assure safe drivers and equipment. Packaging rules tell shippers how to package the materials safely. They also tell drivers how to load, transport and unload the material. To communicate the risk, shippers use hazard warning labels and markings on packages. They also provide shipping papers, emergency response information and placards. These labels and papers communicate the hazard to the shipper, carrier and the driver. To assure safe drivers, anyone who transports hazardous materials must have a commercial driver's license (CDL) and a hazardous materials endorsement. To pass the test for the hazardous materials endorsement, a driver must know how to:
- Identify hazardous materials;
- Safely load shipments;
- Placard a vehicle in accordance with federal regulations;
- Safely transport shipments.

Following regulations

Learn the regulations and follow them. Following the regulations reduces the risk of injury from hazardous materials. Taking shortcuts and breaking the rules is unsafe and could be deadly. Additionally, drivers who violate the regulations can be fined and put in jail. Inspect your vehicle before and during each trip. Police may stop and inspect your vehicle. When stopped, they may check your shipping papers, vehicle placards, the hazardous materials endorsement on your driver's license and your knowledge of hazardous materials.

Licensing and endorsements

You must have a commercial driver's license (CDL) with a hazardous materials endorsement to drive a vehicle carrying hazardous materials that requires placards. You must pass a written test to get this endorsement. Everything you need to know to pass the written test is in this section. However, this is just the beginning. You can learn more by reading the federal and state regulations for hazardous materials and by attending training courses.

Training requirements

Hazardous materials courses are usually offered by your employer, colleges, universities and associations. In fact, the federal regulations require training and testing for all drivers who transport hazardous materials. You must be trained and tested at least once every 3 years. Your employer must provide this training and testing. Your employer must also keep a record of the training completed by each employee who works with hazardous materials. Federal regulations also require that drivers receive special training before driving a vehicle transporting certain flammable gas materials or highway/route-controlled radioactive materials. Drivers transporting cargo tanks and portable tanks must also receive specialized training. Your employer must provide this training.

Permits

The majority of states and some localities require registrations or permits to transport hazardous material or subsets of such materials. States and counties may also require drivers to follow special hazardous materials routes. The federal government may require permits or exemptions for special hazardous materials cargo such as rocket fuel. Find out about permits, exemptions and special routes for the places that you drive.

Roles in transporting hazardous materials

The shipper sends hazardous products from one place to another by truck, rail, ship or airplane. The shipper:
- Uses hazardous materials regulations to determine the product's:
  - proper shipping name
  - hazard class
  - identification number
  - correct packaging
  - correct label and markings
  - correct placards
- Prepares products for shipping. The shipper:
  - packages, marks and labels all materials;
  - prepares shipping papers;
  - provides emergency response information;
  - supplies placards.
- Certifies on the shipping paper that the shipment has been prepared according to federal regulations. If you are pulling cargo tanks supplied by you or your employer, the certification statement is not required.

The carrier is a person or company engaged in the transportation of passengers or property as a for-hire or private carrier. The carrier:
- Takes the shipment from the shipper to its destination.
- Refuses improper shipments.
- Reports accidents and incidents involving hazardous materials to the proper government agency.

The driver safely transports the shipment without delay. The driver:
- Makes sure the shipper has identified, marked and labeled the hazardous materials.
- Refuses leaking packages and shipments.
- Placards his vehicle when loading, if required.
- Follows all regulations about transporting hazardous materials.
- Keeps hazardous materials shipping papers and emergency response information in the proper place.

Communication rules

A material's hazard class shows the risks associated with it. There are 9 different hazard classes. The chart below gives the meaning of each hazard class and lists the types of materials included in each class.

Class	Division	Name of Class or Division	Example
1	1.1 1.2 1.3 1.4 1.5 1.6	Explosives (Mass Detonations) Projection Hazards Mass Fire Hazards Minor Hazards Very Insensitive Extremely Insensitive	Dynamite Ammunition for Cannons Display Fireworks Small Arms Ammunition Blasting Agents Explosive Devices
2	2.1 2.2 2.3	Flammable Gases Non-Flammable Gases Poisonous/Toxic Gases	Propane Helium Fluorine, Compressed
3	---	Flammable Liquids	Gasoline, Diesel Fuel
4	4.1 4.2 4.3	Flammable Solids Spontaneous Combustible Dangerous When Wet	Ammonium Picrate, Wetted White Phosphorus Sodium
5	5.1 5.2	Oxidizers Organic Peroxides	Ammonium Nitrate Methyl Ethyl Ketone Peroxide
6	6.1 6.2	Poison (Toxic Material) Infectious Substances	Potassium Cyanide Anthrax Virus
7	---	Radioactive	Uranium
8	---	Corrosives	Battery Fluid
9	---	Miscellaneous Hazardous Materials	Polychlorinated Biphenyls (PCB)
None		ORM-D (Other Regulated Material-Domestic)	Food Flavorings, Medicines, Cleaning Compounds, and Other Consumer Commodities
None	---	Combustible Liquids	Fuel Oil

Hazardous Materials Table in the federal regulations:
- Appendix A to the Hazardous Materials Table-the List of Hazardous Substances and Reportable Quantities, and
- Appendix B to the Hazardous Materials Table-the List of Marine Pollutants
- Before transporting a material, look for its name on these three lists. Some materials may be on all lists. Others may be on only one.

Appendix A-List of Hazardous Substances and Reportable Quantities the Department of Transportation (DOT) and the Environmental Protection Agency (EPA) want to know about spills of hazardous substances. These substances are named in **Appendix A of the federal regulations** Part of this list is shown below.

The name Phosgene is starred (*) because the name also appears in the hazardous materials table.

Spills of 10 pounds or more must be reported.

LIST OF HAZARDOUS SUBSTANCES AND REPORTABLE QUANTITIES - Continued

Hazardous Substance	Other Names That the Product May Be Called	Reportable Quantity (RQ) Pounds (Kilograms)
Phenyl mercaptan @	Benzinethiol Thiophenol*	100 (45.4)
Phenylmercuric acetate	Mercury, (acetato-0) phenyl	100 (45.4)
N-Phenylthiourea	Thiourea, phenyl	100 (45.4)
Phorate	Phosphorodithioic acid, O,O-diethyl S-(ethylthio), methylester	
Phosgene*	Carbonyl chloride	10 (4.54)
Phosphine*	Hydrogen Phosphide	10 (4.54)
Phosphoric acid*		100 (45.4)
Phosphroic acid, diethyl		5000 (2270)
4-nitrophenyl ester	Diethyl-p nitrophenyl phosphate	100 (45.4)
Phosphoric acid, lead salt	Lead phosphate	1 (0.454)

- Column 1 shows names of elements and compounds that are hazardous substances.
- Column 2 shows other names that these substances may be called.
- Column 3 shows the reportable quantity for each product. If you spill this amount of the material or more, you or your employer must report the spill. Packages that contain a reportable quantity of the material will show the letters RQ. The letters RQ will also show on the shipping paper.
- If the words INHALATION HAZARD appear on the shipping paper or package, you must use the POISON or POISON GAS placards. These placards must be used in addition to other placards required by the product's hazard class. Always display the hazard class and the POISON placards even for small amounts.
- Appendix B-Shows the lists of marine pollutants.
- Communication Rules

Shipping papers
A shipping paper describes the hazardous materials being transported. Shipping papers include shipping orders, bills of lading and manifests. After an accident or hazardous materials accident or spill, you may be injured and unable to tell others about your hazardous cargo. Firefighters and police can prevent or reduce the amount of damage and injury if they know about the hazardous materials you are carrying. Your life and the lives of others could depend on quickly locating hazardous materials shipping papers. Shippers must describe hazardous materials correctly and include an emergency response telephone number on the shipping papers. Carriers and drivers must tab hazardous materials shipping papers or keep them on top of other shipping papers. They must also keep the emergency response information with the shipping papers. Drivers must keep hazardous materials shipping papers:
- In a pouch on the driver's door, or
- In clear view within immediate reach while the driver's seat belt is fastened, or
- On the driver's seat when the driver is out of the vehicle or in a pouch on the driver's door.

The shipping paper shown below describes a shipment:

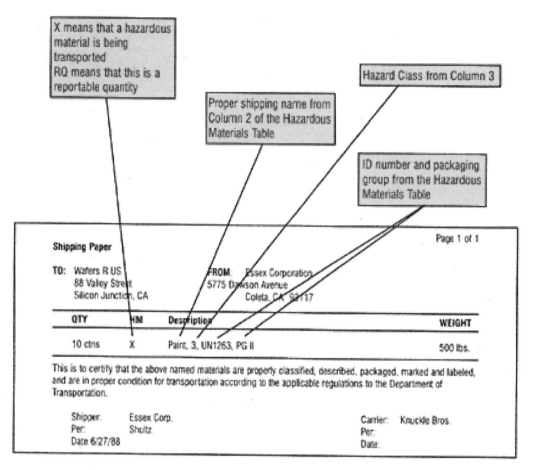

A shipping paper for hazardous materials must include:
- page numbers if the shipping paper has more than one page. The first page must show the total number of pages. For example, "page 1 of 4."
- a proper shipping description for each hazardous material. See below for a list of items in the shipping description.
- a shipper's certification signed by the shipper. This certification states that the shipper prepared the shipment according to the federal regulations.

If the shipping paper describes hazardous and non-hazardous products, the hazardous materials will be:
- described first, or
- highlighted in a contrasting color, or
- identified by an X placed before the shipping name in a column labeled HM. If a reportable quantity is present in one package, the letters RQ may be used instead of X.

Package labels
Package labels are diamond-shaped hazard warning labels found on most hazardous materials packages. These labels inform others of the hazard. If the diamond label does not fit on the package, shippers may put the label on a tag attached to the package. For example, compressed gas cylinders often have tags or decals.

Placards
Placards warn others of hazardous materials. They are placed on the outside of the vehicle and identify the hazard class of the cargo. A placarded vehicle must have at least 4 identical placards. Placards must be readable from all four directions. Therefore, they are put on the front, rear and both sides of the vehicle. Placards measure 10 ¾ inches square and are turned in a diamond shape. Cargo tanks and other bulk packaging display the identification number of their contents on placards. Or they may use orange panels or white diamond-shape displays the same size as placards. Shippers, carriers and drivers use three lists to identify hazardous materials.

Shipping description

The shipping description for a hazardous material includes (in this order):
- proper shipping name
- hazard class or division
- the identification number
- the packing group-the group is displayed in Roman numerals (for example, I, II, III). The numerals may be preceded by the letters PG.
- Shipping name, hazard class and ID number must not be abbreviated unless authorized in the federal regulations. The description must also show:
- The total quantity of each hazardous product and the unit of measure (for example, pounds). Total quantity must appear before or after the basic description. The packaging type and unit of measure may be abbreviated. For example:
  - 10 ctns. Paint, 3, UN1263, PG II, 500 lbs.
- The letters RQ if a reportable quantity is present,
- The name of the hazardous substance if the letters RQ appear,
- For n.o.s. (not otherwise specified) and generic descriptions, the technical name of the hazardous material must be shown. For example, weed killer is a generic name. The technical name is paraquat.
- The shipper of hazardous wastes must put the word WASTE before the name of the material on the shipping paper (hazardous waste manifest). For example:
  - Waste Acetone, 3, PGII, UN1090, PG II
- You may not use a hazard class or ID number to describe a non-hazardous material.
- Shippers must list an emergency response telephone number on the shipping paper. The number can be used by emergency workers to get information about any hazardous materials involved in a spill or fire.
- Shippers must also provide emergency response information to the motor carrier for each hazardous material being shipped. The driver must carry this information. You must be able to use this information away from the motor vehicle and it must provide information on how to safely handle incidents involving the materials shipped. It must include the shipping name of the hazardous material and information about the risks of fire and explosion and risks to health. It must also include information about initial methods for handling fires, spills and leaks of materials.
- The emergency information may be included on the shipping paper or another document that includes the basic description and technical name of the hazardous material. Or, it may be in a guidance book such as the Emergency Response Guide (ERG). The driver must provide the emergency response information to any federal, state or local authority responding to or investigating a hazardous materials incident.

A hazard class indicates the general nature of the hazard. Within some classes, divisions exist to indicate additional hazards. For example, Class 2 covers all compressed gases. Within Class 2:
- Division 2.1 = Flammable Gas
- Division 2.2 = Nonflammable Gas
- Division 2.3 = Poison Gas

Certification statement

When the shipper packages hazardous materials, he certifies that the package has been prepared according federal regulations. The signed shipper's certification appears on the original shipping paper. Exceptions: A shipper does not have to sign a certification statement if the shipper is a private carrier transporting its own product and the product will not be transported by another carrier. The shipper does not have to sign a certification statement if the material is transported in a cargo tank supplied by the carrier. Unless a package is clearly unsafe, you may accept the shipper's certification concerning proper packaging. Some carriers have additional rules about transporting hazardous materials. Follow your employer's rules when accepting shipments.

Package markings and labels

Shippers print required markings directly on the package, an attached label or tag. The most important package marking is the name of the hazardous material. It is the same name as the one used on the shipping paper. The shipper will put the following information on the package:
- The name and address of the shipper or consignee (the business or person to whom the shipment is being sent)
- The hazardous material's shipping name and identification number

Required labels
If a reportable quantity or inhalation hazardous is being shipped, the shipper will also put RQ or INHALATION HAZARD on the package. Packages with liquid containers inside will have arrows pointing in the corrected upright direction. The labels used always reflect the hazard class of the product. Labels should appear near the proper shipping name.

Recognizing hazardous materials
Learn to recognize shipments of hazardous materials. To find out if the shipment includes hazardous materials, look for these clues:
- An entry with a proper shipping name, hazard class and ID number.
- A highlighted entry or one with an X or RQ in the hazardous materials column.
- Look for other clues and ask:
  - What business is the shipper in? Paint dealers, chemical suppliers, scientific supply houses, pest control or agricultural suppliers, explosives, munitions or fireworks dealers are all likely sources for hazardous materials.
  - Do you see tanks with diamond labels or placards around the business?
  - What type of package is being shipped? Cylinders and drums are often used for hazardous materials shipments.
  - Is a hazard class label, proper shipping name and ID number on the package?
  - Does the package have handling precautions?

Hazardous waste manifest
When transporting hazardous wastes, you must sign and carry a Uniform Hazardous Waste Manifest. The name and EPA identification number of the shippers, carriers and destination must appear on the manifest. Shippers must prepare, date and sign the manifest. Treat the manifest as a shipping paper when transporting the waste. Only give the waste shipment to a carrier with an EPA identification number or an EPA permitted treatment, storage or disposal facility. Each carrier/driver transporting the shipment must sign the manifest. After you deliver the shipment, keep your copy of the manifest. Each copy must have all needed signatures and dates. It must include the signature of the person to whom you delivered the waste.

Placarding

Attach the appropriate placards to the vehicle before you drive it. If you find that your vehicle is not placarded or placarded improperly, you may move it only during an emergency to protect life or property. To decide which placards to use, you must know:

- The hazard class of the materials.
- The amount of hazardous materials shipped.
- The total weight of all hazardous materials in your vehicle.

Placard tables: There are two placard tables that tell you how to placard your vehicle.

- Placard Table 1 - Any Amount. Table 1 materials must be placarded whenever any amount is transported.
-

IF YOUR VEHICLE CONTAINS ANY AMOUNT OF:	PLACARD as:
1.1	EXPLOSIVE 1.1
1.2	EXPLOSIVE 1.2
1.3	EXPLOSIVE 1.3
2.3	POISON GAS
4.3	DANGEROUS WHEN WET
6.1 (PG 1, inhalation hazard only)	POISON, INHALATION HAZARD REF.
7 (Radioactive Yellow III label only)	172.55c
	RADIOACTIVE

- Placard Table 2-1,001 lbs or more. Except for bulk packaging, the hazard classes in Table 2 need placards only if the total amount transported weighs 1,001 lbs or more including the package. To find out if you need a placard, add the amounts from all shipping papers for all the Table 2 products that you have on board.

CATEGORY OF MATERIAL (Hazard class or division number and description as appropriate)	PLACARD NAME
1.4	EXPLOSIVES 1.4
1.5	EXPLOSIVES 1.5
1.6	EXPLOSIVES 1.6
2.1	FLAMMABLE GAS
3	FLAMMABLE
Combustible liquid	COMBUSTIBLE
4.1	FLAMMABLE SOLID
4.2	SPONTANEOUS COMBUSTIBLE
5.1	OXIDIZER
5.2	ORGANIC PEROXIDE
6.1 (PG I or II, other than PG I inhalation hazard) If ZONE A or B	POISON INHALATION
6.1 (PG III)	KEEP AWAY FROM FOOD
6.2	(no placard required)
8	CORROSIVE
8	CLASS 9**
ORM-D	(no placard required)

- You may use DANGEROUS placards instead of separate placards for each Table 2 hazard class if:
  - you have loaded two or more Table 2 hazard classes that weigh 1,001 lbs. or more and which require different placards, and
  - you have not loaded 2205 lbs. or more of any Table 2 hazard class material from any one shipper.
  - If you have loaded 2205 lbs. or more of a hazardous material from anyone shipper, you must use the specific placard for this material
- If the words INHALATION HAZARD are on the shipping paper or package, you must display POISON or POISON GAS placards, as appropriate, in addition to other placards required by the products hazard class.
- If the vehicle contains division 1.1 or 1.2 explosives and is placarded with EXPLOSIVES 1.1 or EXPLOSIVES 1.2 and you are also carrying EXPLOSIVES 1.5, OXIDIZER or DANGEROUS placard materials - you may use DANGEROUS placards instead of separate placards for each Table 2 Hazard you have loaded.
- If the vehicle displays a Division 2.1 FLAMMABLE GAS or a Division 2.2 OXYGEN placard, you do not need to use a Division 2.2 NON-FLAMMABLE GAS placard.
- Placards that identify the primary hazard class of a material must show the hazard class or division number in the lower corner of the placard. Placards that identify a secondary hazard class of a material may not show the hazard class or division number.
- You may display a placard for a hazardous material, even if it is not required, as long as the placard identifies the hazard of the material being transported.

Loading and unloading hazardous materials

General loading requirements
- Do everything you can to protect containers of hazardous materials. Don't use tools which might damage containers or packaging during loading. Don't use hooks.
- Before loading or unloading, set the parking brake. Make sure the vehicle will not move.
- Many products become more hazardous when exposed to heat. Load hazardous materials away from heat sources.
- Watch for signs of leaking or damaged containers. Leaks spell trouble! Do not transport leaking packages. You, your truck and others could be in danger.
- To prevent movement during transit, brace packages containing:
  - Class 1 (explosives)
  - Class 2 (gases)
  - Class 3 (flammable liquids)
  - Class 4 (flammable solids)
  - Class 5 (oxidizers)
  - Division 6.1 (poisons)
  - Class 8 (corrosives)
- No smoking! When loading or unloading hazardous materials, keep fire away. Don't let people smoke nearby.
- Never smoke around:
  - Class 1 (explosives)
  - Division 2.1 (flammable gas)
  - Class 4 (flammable solids)
  - Class 5 (oxidizers)
  - Class 3 (flammables)
- Brace containers so they will not fall, slide or bounce during transit. Be careful when loading containers with valves or other fittings.
- After loading, do not open any package during your trip. Never transfer hazardous materials from one package to another during the trip. You may empty a cargo tank, but do not empty any other package while it is on the vehicle.

- Cargo heater rules: There are special cargo heater regulations for loading:
  - Class 1 (explosives)
  - Class 3 (flammable liquids)
  - Division 2.1 (flammable gas)

These rules are found in the Code of Federal Regulations:
- The regulations generally forbid use of cargo heaters, including automatic cargo heating/refrigeration units. Unless you have read all the related regulations, do not load these products in a cargo space that has a heater.
- Use closed cargo space: You cannot have overhang or tailgate loads of these materials:
  - Class 1 (explosives)
  - Class 4 (flammable solids)
  - Class 5 (oxidizers)

You must load these hazardous materials in a closed cargo space unless all packages are:
  - fire and water resistant, or
  - covered with a fire and water-resistant tarp.

Precautions for specific hazards
Explosives:
- Turn off your engine before loading or unloading explosives. Then check the cargo space. You must:
  - Disable cargo heaters. Disconnect heater power sources and drain heater fuel tanks.
  - Make sure there are no sharp points that might damage cargo. Look for bolts, screws, nails, broken side panels and broken floor boards.
  - Use a floor lining with Division 1.1, 1.2 or .1.3 explosives. The floors must be tight and the liner must be either non-metallic material or non-ferrous metal (metal that does not contain iron).
- Use extra care to protect explosives. Never use hooks or other metal tools. Never drop, throw or roll packages. Protect explosive packages from other cargo that might cause damage.
- Do not transfer a Division 1.1, 1.2 or 1.3 explosive from one vehicle to another on a public roadway except in an emergency. If you must make an emergency transfer, set out red warning reflectors, flags or electric lanterns. You must warn others on the road.
- Never transport damaged packages of explosives. Do not take a package that shows dampness or an oily stain.
- Do not transport Division 1.1 or 1.2 explosives in vehicle combinations or triples if:
  - A marked or placarded cargo tank is in the combination, or
  - The other vehicle in the combination contains:
    - Division 1.1 A (initiating) explosives
    - Packages of Class 7 (radioactive) materials labeled "Yellow III,"
    - Division 2.3 (poisonous gas) or Division 6.1 (poisonous) materials
    - Hazardous materials in a portable tank, a DOT Spec 106A or 110A tank.

Class 8 (corrosive) materials:

- If loading by hand, load breakable containers of corrosive liquid one by one. Keep them right side up. Do not drop or roll the containers. Load them on an even floor surface. Stack carboys only if the lower tiers can bear the weight of the upper tiers safely. (Carboys are portable tanks that may be metal or plastic and are placed in a special cage.)
- Do not load nitric acid above any other product or stack more than 2 high.
- Load charged storage batteries so their liquid won't spill. Keep them right side up. Make sure other cargo won't fall against or short circuit them.
- Never load corrosive liquids next to or above:
  - Division 1.4
  - Class 4 (flammable solids)
  - Class 5 (oxidizers)
  - Division 2.3, Zone B gases
- Never load corrosive liquids with:
  - Division 1.1 or 1.2
  - Division 1.2 or 1.3
  - Division 1.5 (blasting agents)
  - Division 2.3, Zone A, gases
  - Division 4.2 (spontaneously combustible materials)
  - Division 6.1, PGI, Zone A (poison liquids)
- Class 2 (compressed gasses) including cryogenic liquids. Cryogenic liquids are liquids carried at very cold temperatures. See 49CFR177 for additional details.
  - If your vehicle doesn't have racks to hold cylinders, the cargo space floor must be flat. The cylinders must be:
    - Held upright or braced laying down flat, or
    - In racks attached to the vehicle, or
    - In boxes that will keep them from turning over.
- Division 2.3 (poisonous gas) or Division 6.1 (poisonous) materials
  - Never transport these materials in containers with interconnections
  - Never load a package labeled POISON or POISON GAS in the driver's cab, sleeper or with food material for human or animal consumption.
- Class 7 (radioactive) materials. Some packages of Class 7 (radioactive) materials show a number called the transport index. The shipper labels these packages Radioactive II or Radioactive III and prints the package's transport index on the label.
- Radiation surrounds each package and passes through all nearby packages. As a result, the number of packages you can load together is controlled. Their closeness to people, animals and exposed film is also controlled.
- The transport index (shown below) shows how close you can load Class 7 (radioactive) materials to people, animals or film. For example, you can't leave a package with a transport index of 1.1 within 2 feet of people or cargo space walls during transit. The total transport index of all packages in a single vehicle must not exceed 50. Single vehicles include automobiles, vans, trucks tractors and semi-trailers.

TOTAL TRANSPORT INDEX	MINIMUM DISTANCE IN FEET TO NEAREST UNDEVELOPED FILM					TO PEOPLE OR CARGO COMPARTMENT PARTITIONS
	0-2 Hours	2-4 Hours	4-8 Hours	8-12 Hours	Over 12 Hours	
None	0	0	0	0	0	0
01. to 1.0	1	2	3	4	5	0
1.1 to 5.0	3	4	6	8	11	2
5.1 to 10.0	4	6	9	11	15	3
10.1 to 20.0	5	8	9	11	15	3
20.1 to 30.0	7	10	15	20	29	5
30.1 to 40.0	8	11	17	22	33	6
40.1	9	12	19	24	36	

Radioactive Transport Index
(You will not be tested on this table).

Do not leave radioactive yellow-II or yellow-III labeled packages near people, animals of film longer than shown in this table.

Federal regulations require that some products be loaded separately. You cannot load them together in the same cargo space. The table below lists some examples. The Segregation and Separation chart in the federal regulations names other materials that you must keep apart.

DO NOT LOAD...	IN THE SAME VEHICLE WITH...
Division 6.1 or 2.3 POISON or poison gas labeled material	Animal or human food unless the poison package is overpacked in an approved way. Foodstuffs are anything you swallow. However, mouthwash, toothpaste, and skin creams are not foodstuff.
Division 2.3 (poisonous) gas Zone A or Division 6.1 (poisonous) gas Zone A or Division 6.1 (poison) liquids, PGI Zone A	Division 5.1 (oxidizers), Class 3 (Flammable liquids), Class 8 (corrosive liquids) Division 5.2 (organic peroxides), Division 1.1, 1.2, 1.2 (Class A or B) explosives) Division 1.5 (blasting agents) Division 2.1 (flammable gasses), Division 4.1 (flammable solids) Division 4.2 (spontaneously combustible). Division 4.3 (dangerous when wet). See 499CRF177 for additional details.
Charged storage batteries	Division 1.1 Class A (explosives)
Class 1 (detonated primers)	Any other explosives unless in authorized containers or packaging
Division 6.1 (cyanides or cyanide mixtures)	Acids, corrosive materials, or other acidic materials which could release hydrocyanic acid from cyanides. For example: Cyanides, Inorganic, n.o.s. Silver Cyanide Sodium Cyanide
Nitric acid (Class 8)	Other materials unless the nitric acid is not loaded above any other material and not more than two tiers high.

Marking, loading, and unloading packaging

Bulk packaging
Bulk packaging is any packaging in which hazardous materials are loaded with no intermediate form of containment and which:
- As a receptacle for liquid holds 450 liters or 119 gallons or more; or
- As a receptacle for solids holds 400 kilograms/882 pounds or 450 liters/119 gallons or more; or,
- As a receptacle for gas has a water capacity greater than 454 kilograms/1000 pounds (refer to the definition in 49 CFR 173, 115).

Bulk packaging includes transport vehicles and freight containers. A cargo tank is a bulk packaging which is:
- a tank intended primarily for carrying liquids or gases and includes appurtenances, reinforcements, fittings and closures. For "tank" see 49 CFR 178.337-1 or 178-345-1 (c)
- permanently attached to or forms a part of a motor vehicle. If it is not permanently attached to a motor vehicle, it is loaded or unloaded without being removed from the motor vehicle, and,
- not made according to specifications for cylinders, portable tanks, tank cars or multi-unit tank car tanks.

Portable tanks are bulk containers which are permanently attached to a vehicle. The product is loaded or unloaded while the portable tanks are off the vehicle. Many type of cargo tanks are in use. The most common cargo tanks are MC306/406 for flammable liquids and MC331 for Bulk gases. Other liquid hazardous materials must be transported in other types of specification tanks such as MC307/407 or MC312/412.

Markings
You must display the ID number of the hazardous materials in portable tanks, cargo tanks and intermediate bulk packaging containers. ID numbers are shown in column 4 of the Hazardous Materials Table. Federal regulations require black 100 mm (3.9 inch) numbers on orange panels, placards or a white diamond-shaped background if placards are not required. Specification cargo tanks must show retest date markings. In addition, portable tanks:
- Must show the lessee or owner's name.
- Must display the shipping name of the contents on two opposite sides.

The letters of the shipping name must be at least 2 inches tall on portable tanks with capacities of more than 1,000 gallons and 1 inch tall on portable tanks with capacities of less than 1,000 gallons. The ID number must appear on each side and each end of a portable tank or other bulk packaging that holds 1,000 gallons or more. The ID number must appear on two opposite sides if the portable tank holds less than 1,000 gallons. The ID numbers must be visible when the portable tank is on the motor vehicle. If they are not visible, you must display the ID number on both sides and on both ends of the motor vehicle. If the identification numbers cannot be seen from outside the vehicle, additional numbers must be affixed to the exterior-front, rear and both sides.

Tank loading and unloading
The person in charge of loading and unloading a cargo tank must make sure a qualified person is always watching. The person watching must:
- Be alert.
- Have a clear view of the cargo tank.
- Be within 100 feet of the tank. (397.5 D 1)
- Know the hazards of the materials involved.
- Know procedures to follow in an emergency; and,
- Be authorized and able to move the cargo tank.
- Close all manholes and valves before moving a tank of hazardous materials, no matter how small the amount in the tank or how short the distance. Manholes and valves must be closed to prevent leaks.

Flammable liquids
Turn off your engine before loading or unloading any flammable liquids. Run the engine only if you need it to operate a pump. Ground a cargo tank correctly before filling through an open filling hole. Ground the tank before opening the filling hole and maintain the ground until after you close the filling hole.

Compressed gas
Keep liquid discharge valves on a compressed gas tank closed except when loading and unloading. Run the engine only if you need it to operate a pump. If you run your engine, turn it off after transferring the product and before you unhook the hose. Unhook all loading/unloading connections before coupling, uncoupling or moving a chlorine tank. Always chock trailers and semi-trailers to prevent motion when uncoupled from the tractor or power unit.

Parking and driving rules

Parking with Division 1.1, 1.2 or 1.3 explosives
Never park with Division 1.1, 1.2 or 1.3 explosives within 5 feet of the traveled part of the road. Do not park within 300 feet of:
- a bridge, tunnel, or building,
- a place where people gather, or
- an open fire

If you must park, for example to refuel, be as quick as possible. Do not park on private property unless the owner is aware of the danger. Someone must always watch the parked vehicle. You may let someone else watch the vehicle only if it is:
- on the shipper's property,
- on the carrier's property, or
- on the consignee's property

Safe havens
You may leave your vehicle unattended in a safe haven. A safe haven is an approved place for parking unattended vehicles loaded with explosives. Local or state and federal authorities identify areas for safe havens.

Parking a placarded vehicle not carrying Division 1.1, 1.2 or 1.3 explosives
You may park a placarded vehicle (not carrying explosives) within 5 feet of the traveled part of the road only if your work requires it. Move the vehicle as soon as possible. Someone must always watch the vehicle when parked on a public road or shoulder. Do not uncouple a trailer with hazardous materials and leave it on a public street. Do not park within 300 feet of an open fire.

Attending parked vehicles
The person watching a placarded vehicle must:
- Be in the vehicle and awake. He cannot be in the sleeper berth. Or, the person must be within 100 feet of the vehicle and have it within clear view.
- Be aware of the hazards of the materials being transported.
- Know what to do in an emergency, and
- Be able to move the vehicle if needed.

Flares
If you need to use warning devices, use reflective triangles or red electric lights. NEVER use burning signals, such as flares or fuses, around a:
- Tank used for Class 3 (flammable liquids) or Division 2.1 (flammable gas) whether loaded or empty.
- Vehicle loaded with Division 1.1, 1.2 or 1.3 explosives.

Smoking
Do not smoke while driving or within 25 feet of a placarded cargo tank used for Class 3 (flammable liquids) or Division 2.1 (gases). Do not smoke or carry a lighted cigarette, cigar or pipe while driving or within 25 feet of any vehicle which contains:
- Class 1 Explosives
- Class 3 Flammable Liquids
- Class 4 Flammable Solids Class 5 Oxidizers

Refuel with the engine off
Turn off your engine before fueling a motor vehicle carrying hazardous materials. Someone must always be at the nozzle controlling the fuel flow.

Carry a 10 B:C fire extinguisher

The tractor or power unit or placarded vehicles must have a fire extinguisher with a UL rating of 10 B:C or more. Make sure the extinguisher is charged. Know how to operate it

Equipment for chlorine

A driver transporting chlorine in cargo tanks must have an approved gas mask in the vehicle. The driver must also carry an emergency kit for controlling leaks in the dome cover plate fittings on the cargo tank.

Permit and route restrictions

Most states and some localities require permits to transport hazardous materials and wastes. Rules about permits can change. Make sure you have all the needed permits before you start. Many states and localities have either route restrictions or designated routes for the transportation of hazardous materials. These restrictions and designations can change often. If you work for a carrier, ask your dispatcher about route restrictions or permits. If you are an independent trucker and are planning a new route, check with agencies where you plan to travel. Some localities prohibit transportation of hazardous materials through tunnels, over bridges or other roadways. Check before you start. Whenever you drive a placarded vehicle, avoid heavily populated areas, crowds, tunnels, narrow streets and alleys. Take other routes, even if they are more inconvenient. Never drive a placarded vehicle near open fires unless you can safely pass without stopping.

Carrying Division 1.1, 1.2 or 1.3 explosives

If you are carrying Division 1.1, 1.2 or 1.3 explosives:
- You must have a written route plan and follow that plan.
- Keep a copy of the plan with you while transporting the explosives.
- Carriers prepare the route plan ahead of time and give the driver a copy.
- You may plan the route yourself if you pick up the explosives somewhere other than at your employer's terminal. If you plan the route, write it out in advance and keep it with you while transporting the explosives.
- Deliver shipments of explosives only to authorized persons or leave them in locked rooms designed for explosives storage.
- A carrier must choose the safest route to transport placarded radioactive materials. After choosing the route, the carrier must tell the driver about the radioactive materials and tell him the route plan.

Shipping papers and emergency response information

Do not accept a hazardous materials shipment without a properly prepared shipping paper. A shipping paper for hazardous materials must always be easily recognized. Other people must be able to find it quickly after an accident. Put hazardous materials shipping papers on top of your stack of shipping papers or tab them so that they stand out from other papers. When you are driving, keep shipping papers within your reach (with your seat belt on) or in a pouch on the driver's door. They must be seen easily by someone entering the cab. When you are not behind the wheel, leave the shipping papers in the driver's pouch or on the driver's seat. Emergency response information must be kept with the shipping paper.

Papers for Division 1.1, 1.2 or 1.3 explosives

A carrier must give each driver transporting Division 1.1, 1.2 or 1.3 explosives a copy of Federal Motor Carrier Safety Regulations (FMCSR), Part 397. The carrier must also give the driver written instructions about what to do if the driver is delayed or in an accident. These instructions must include:
- Names and telephone numbers of people to contact (including carrier agents or shippers).
- Information about the explosives being transported
- Information about what to do in emergencies such as fires, accidents or leaks.

The driver must sign a receipt for these documents. When you are driving, you must have and be familiar with the:
- shipping papers
- written emergency instructions
- written route plan
- a copy of FMCSR, part 397

Check your tires every 2 hours/100 miles
Make sure your tires are properly inflated before you begin your trip. Check placarded vehicles with dual tires at the start of each trip and when you park. You must stop and check the tires every 2 hours or 100 miles, whichever comes first. Use a tire pressure gauge to check the pressure. This is the only acceptable way to check pressure. Do not drive with a tire that is leaking or flat except to the nearest safe place to fix it. Remove any overheated tire. Place it a safe distance from your vehicle. Don't drive until you correct the cause of overheating. Follow the rules about parking and attending placarded vehicles. They apply even when you are checking, repairing or replacing tires.

Stop before railroad crossings (392.10)
Stop before a railroad crossing if your vehicle:
- is placarded
- carries any amount of chlorine
- is a cargo tank used for hazardous materials, whether empty or loaded

You must stop 15 to 50 feet before the nearest rail. Proceed only when you are sure that no train is coming. Don't shift gears while crossing the tracks.

Hazardous Materials Endorsement Tests

Part One

1. Which must be shown on a hazardous materials bill of lading?
   a. The shipper's permit number
   b. The quantity of hazardous materials
   c. All of the carrier's state and federal permit numbers

2. What are placards?
   a. Diamond-shaped warning signs placed on vehicles
   b. Warning signs that are placed on boxes and other packages
   c. Stickers that must be displayed in the lower right side of windshields

3. Before transporting certain radioactive materials a route restriction?
   a. May be required if the shipper tells you about it
   b. Should be obtained
   c. May be necessary

4. Which is correct about listing hazardous materials on a bill of lading?
   a. The commodity is named in the hazardous materials column.
   b. All commodities must be named with large letters.
   c. The proper shipping name of the commodity is listed first.

5. What is the intent of the hazardous materials regulations?
   a. To communicate risk, to protect all, and to contain the product.
   b. To reduce the costs of transportation.
   c. To raise funds for the government through fines for violations.

6. Two letters that may be shown before the name of a hazardous substance?
   a. AD
   b. PX
   c. RQ

7. Which is not part of a correct shipping name?
   a. NOS
   b. The technical name of the product
   c. The brand name of the product

8. Information on a hazardous materials shipping paper must be shown?
   a. Proper shipping name, then packing group, then ID number
   b. Proper shipping name, then hazard class, ID number, packing group
   c. Hazard class first followed by shipping name, ID and packing group

9. Which is not the proper four-digit Identification (ID) Number?
   a. USA number
   b. NA number
   c. UN number

10. If a label will not fit on a hazardous materials package?
    a. The driver may use a bright red marking pen to mark the package.
    b. The package will not have to be labeled if it weighs less than 100 pounds.
    c. The label must be put on a tag which is then wired to the package.

Part Two

1. Which is an acceptable method of showing shipper's certification on papers?
   a. Longhand
   b. Printed
   c. Red Ink

2. Drivers who transport highway route-controlled radioactive materials must have?
   a. Had special training within the past two years
   b. Special training from their local union every three years
   c. Special training before each trip

3. Which is an acceptable quantity shown on a hazardous materials bill of lading?
   a. 2,100 pounds
   b. 2100
   c. 2,100

4. In bulk quantities only on highways marine pollutants are regulated?
   a. In interstate commerce
   b. In foreign commerce within all countries
   c. In intrastate and interstate commerce

5. You may load cylinders of compressed gas without racks if the cylinders?
   a. Can be loaded in rounded containers
   b. Can be loaded in an upright position without supports
   c. Can be loaded on the vehicle laying down flat and braced

6. A vehicle carrying hazardous materials must be parked at least?
   a. 300 feet away from an open fire
   b. 600 feet away from an open fire
   c. 900 feet away from an open fire

7. When placards are required, they should be placed?
   a. On the rear and both sides of the vehicle
   b. On the front, the rear, and both sides of the vehicle
   c. As long as four placards are displayed they may be placed as wanted

8. The Hazardous Materials Table is organized?
   a. In alphabetical order by the proper shipping name
   b. In numerical order by the hazard class number only
   c. In the same order as the listings in the placard tables

9. With tank vehicles the Identification (ID) Number must appear on?
   a. The tanks and the placards.
   b. The shipping papers.
   c. The placards and the shipping papers.

10. When a vehicle is parked the hazardous material shipping papers must be?
   a. Kept on the seat or in a pocket in the left door
   b. Kept under the seat
   c. In the glove compartment or in the driver's possession

Part Three

1. Labels on hazardous materials must measure?
    a. At least two inches on each side
    b. At least three inches on each side
    c. At least four inches on each side

2. If a shipper's certification is signed, must you accept a leaking package?
    a. You must accept the package, but report it to your dispatcher immediately.
    b. You must refuse the shipment.
    c. You must place the shipment inside a larger container that is not leaking.

3. Which word is a hazardous class description found on labels?
    a. Corrosive
    b. Fragile
    c. Cancer

4. If required to stop for a railroad crossing you must stop?
    a. Twenty to forty feet before the nearest rail
    b. Fifteen to fifty feet before the nearest rail
    c. Wherever you can plainly see any approaching train

5. Corrosives could require more than one label because they could also be?
    a. Asbestos
    b. Cancer-inducing in rats
    c. Poison by inhalation

6. A commodity named in Placard Table I requires a placard for?
    a. Any quantity
    b. A shipment that weighs more than a thousand pounds
    c. A shipment that contains more than one class of hazardous materials

7. What is a marking that must be shown on liquid hazardous materials packages?
    a. This Side Up
    b. This Package May Leak
    c. This package Opens at the Bottom

8. For the placards to use with packaged freight you must know the hazard class?
    a. The amount shipped and the total weight of hazardous materials on board
    b. The amount shipped and the ID Number
    c. The amount shipped, the ID Number and the NMFC classification

9. Which of these is true?
    a. With hazardous materials there are no regulations against smoking.
    b. You may smoke around Flammables if there is a fire extinguisher handy.
    c. Do not smoke when around Explosives, Flammables and Oxidizers.

10. When fueling a placarded vehicle, someone must be?
    a. Supervising the fueling from a safe distance
    b. Supervising the fueling from at least 25 feet away
    c. At the nozzle, controlling the fuel flow

Part Four

1. Which Code of Federal Regulations requires that placards be used?
   a. Title 13, CFR
   b. Title 27, CFR
   c. Title 49, CFR

2. When should a driver have all needed placards in place for packaged freight?
   a. Before loading
   b. After loading each commodity that requires a certain placard
   c. After the vehicle is loaded but before it goes out onto the highway

3. How should each trailer be placarded in a combination unit?
   a. At the front of the first trailer and the back of the last trailer
   b. For the class of hazardous material contained in that trailer
   c. On the sides of the trailers only with a placard on the power unit

4. When are you allowed to have overhang (tailgate) loads of Explosives?
   a. Never
   b. When there are two escort vehicles with one following
   c. During daylight hours and the overhang does not exceed five feet

5. An exception to the rule for trailer placarding for semis is?
   a. There is no exception to the rule that trailers must be placarded all around.
   b. Instead of the trailer, a placard may be placed on the front of the tractor.
   c. At least one placard must be placed on the front of any semi trailer.

6. Which requires a placard even if there is only one pound of it on board?
   a. Flammable Liquids
   b. Corrosives
   c. Class A Explosives

7. What placard may be used for Table 2 materials none of which equal 1,000 lbs?
   a. Dangerous
   b. Dangerous When Wet
   c. Hazardous

8. When driving a placarded vehicle you must stop and check the tires?
   a. Every 200 miles
   b. Every two hours or 100 miles
   c. Every hour or 55 miles

9. Cargo tanks or portable tanks loaded with hazardous materials must show?
   a. The ID Number of the product
   b. A label on each side
   c. Warning: Flammable

10. The total transport index of all radioactive packages in a vehicle can't exceed?
    a. 25
    b. 50
    c. 100

Part Five

1. An X or an RQ shown in the HM column of a shipping paper means?
   a. The material in the shipment is a hazardous material.
   b. This is a hazardous material that any driver can transport.
   c. This material is an exception to the hazardous material rules.

2. If special permits or special routes are required, who is responsible for this?
   a. Owner of the vehicle
   b. The company dispatcher
   c. Driver of the vehicle

3. The EPA registration numbers of the carrier, shipper and destination must be on?
   a. All bills of lading
   b. Material Safety Data Sheets
   c. Hazardous Waste Manifests

4. Transporters must keep a copy of hazardous waste manifests for at least?
   a. One year
   b. Two years
   c. Three years

5. Which may be exempt from labeling rules when transported in small quantities?
   a. Consumer products
   b. Class A Explosives
   c. Poison Gas

6. A driver should count the total number of packages loaded and should count?
   a. The number of damaged packages
   b. The number of packages with reinforcement
   c. The number of packages of hazardous materials.

7. Poisons must not be transported with which of the following?
   a. Carcinogens
   b. Foods, animal feed or medicines
   c. Fungicides, pesticides or liquid fertilizers

8. What is a way to determine if two materials are not compatible to transport?
   a. Study the charts that are available.
   b. Use the trial and error method.
   c. Phone the local police or sheriff's office.

9. A driver transporting hazardous materials should keep those materials?
   a. Away from other packages
   b. Away from moisture
   c. Away from walls or side racks

10. What is the status of vehicle brakes when hazardous materials are being loaded?
    a. All brakes should be released.
    b. The parking brakes should be set.
    c. All brakes should be locked.

Answer Key

Part One

1. B: The quantity of hazardous materials
2. A: Diamond-shaped warning signs placed on vehicles
3. C: May be necessary
4. C: The proper shipping name of the commodity is listed first.
5. A: To communicate risk, to protect all, and to contain the product.
6. C: RQ
7. C: The brand name of the product
8. B: Proper shipping name, then hazard class, ID number, packing group
9. A: USA number
10. C: The label must be put on a tag which is then wired to the package.

Part Two

1. B: Printed
2. A: Had special training within the past two years
3. A: 2,100 pounds
4. C: In intrastate and interstate commerce
5. C: Can be loaded on the vehicle laying down flat and braced
6. A: 300 feet away from an open fire
7. B: On the front, the rear, and both sides of the vehicle
8. A: In alphabetical order by the proper shipping name
9. C: The placards and the shipping papers.
10. A: Kept on the seat or in a pocket in the left door

Part Three

1. C: At least four inches on each side
2. B: You must refuse the shipment.
3. A: Corrosive
4. B: Fifteen to fifty feet before the nearest rail
5. C: Poison by inhalation
6. A: Any quantity
7. A: This Side Up
8. A: The amount shipped and the total weight of hazardous materials on board
9. C: Do not smoke when around Explosives, Flammables and Oxidizers.
10. C: At the nozzle, controlling the fuel flow

Part Four

1. C: Title 49, CFR
2. C: After the vehicle is loaded but before it goes out onto the highway
3. B: For the class of hazardous material contained in that trailer
4. A: Never
5. B: Instead of the trailer, a placard may be placed on the front of the tractor.
6. C: Class A Explosives
7. A: Dangerous
8. B: Every two hours or 100 miles
9. A: The ID Number of the product
10. B: 50

Part Five

1. A: The material in the shipment is a hazardous material.
2. C: Driver of the vehicle
3. C: Hazardous Waste Manifests
4. C: Three years
5. A: Consumer products
6. C: The number of packages of hazardous materials.
7. B: Foods, animal feed or medicines
8. A: Study the charts that are available.
9. B: Away from moisture
10. B: The parking brakes should be set.

Passenger and School Bus Endorsements

School buses

To drive a school bus, you must be at least 18 years of age. You must also hold a valid commercial driver's license. Depending on the weight and size of the bus that you will drive, you will be issued a Class B or Class C license. Additionally you must have a passenger bus endorsement and a school bus endorsement on your CDL. School bus endorsements are not transferable from state to state. To get your CDL and the endorsements to drive a school bus, you must pass:
- the written general knowledge test
- the written passenger bus test
- the written school bus test
- the written air brakes test if your vehicle is equipped with air brakes;
- the skills test required for the class of vehicle that you plan to drive. If you plan to drive a bus equipped with air brakes, you must take the skills test in a bus equipped with air brakes.

To prepare for these tests, study:
- General Knowledge
- Air Brakes (if your vehicle will be equipped with air brakes)
- School Buses (this section)
- Transporting Passengers

If you plan to drive a school bus designed to carry fewer than 16 passengers, including the driver, you do not need to obtain a CDL, Class B or C, or the passenger bus endorsement. However, you must have the school bus endorsement on your driver's license. Therefore, you will need to take the school bus knowledge and skills tests. You will be restricted to driving buses designed to carry fewer than 16 passengers and this restriction will be printed on your license.

Operating the Bus Safely

Loading and unloading passengers

Turn on your school bus traffic warning lights:
- You must turn on the warning lights before you stop to load or unload students.
- If the posted speed limit is less than 35 mph, turn on the warning lights at least 100 feet before the stop.
- If the posted speed is 35 mph or more, turn on the warning lights at least 200 feet before the stop.
- Do not use the warning lights except when loading and unloading

Extend the warning sign and crossing control arm only when the bus is stopped to load and unload passengers.

When loading or unloading students:
- Do not use the emergency four-way hazard flashers.
- Stop in the right lane of the road.
- On divided highways, five lane roads where the middle lane is used for turning, or heavily traveled roads, unload the students on the side of the road where they live.
- Stop only when the bus can be seen clearly at a safe distance.
- Make sure all students are on the bus and seated before moving.
- Before backing the bus, make sure all students are on the bus and seated.
- When unloading, make sure all students are clear of the bus before moving. Most injuries occur when the bus is stopped to load or unload students.
- Never park the bus so that the emergency exit will be blocked while students are on board.
- Report drivers who illegally pass a bus stopped to load or unload passengers. Make a note of:
  - the license plate number and state
  - the make, type and color of the vehicle
  - date, time and location of the incident

Backing the bus

Do not back the bus unless there is no other safe way to move the vehicle. Drive around the block or make a detour rather than backing the bus. Pick up passengers before backing or turning. Post a lookout on the inside, back of the bus to warn of obstacles, approaching persons or other vehicles. Check your mirrors constantly while backing. Unload passengers after backing or turning.

Passing and turning

Do not pass or run side-by-side with another bus on the highway. Keep a safe distance between vehicles if you must pass. When turning left, get into the left lane (if there is one) in plenty of time to make the turn safely.

Following other vehicles

Always leave at least a bus length between you and the vehicle in front of you.
Outside of cities and towns, keep at least 200 feet between you and the vehicle in front of you.

Railroad crossings

As you approach a railroad crossing, tap your brakes lightly to warn other drivers that the bus is about to stop. Turn on your four-way hazard lights. Come to a full stop 15 to 50 feet from the nearest rail. Open the entrance door and driver's window. Turn off the warning lights unless you are loading and unloading passengers. Listen and look carefully in both directions. When it is safe to cross, close the entrance door and turn off the four-way hazard lights. Cross the railroad tracks in a gear which allows you to cross the rails completely without changing gears.

Speed limits for buses

When traveling on interstate highways, you may drive 55 mph. You must travel 35 mph or less on all other highways. If you are driving on a highway where the posted speed limit is 45 mph or higher and you are not loading or unloading passengers between your place of departure and your destination, you may travel 45 mph. 25 mph in school, business and residential areas. Remember, weather, road and traffic conditions may require you to travel slower than these speed limits. When in doubt, slow down.

Handling Emergencies

Emergency drills

Most State laws require that you hold an emergency exit drill at least once during the first 90 calendar days of the school year or more often if needed. Your local school board or board of education may require more frequent drills.

Emergency situations

Bus accidents
- Do not move the bus until police or school officials arrive.
- Check the bus for injured students.
- Protect the crash scene by setting out flares or reflectors.
- Do not leave students unattended. Have a responsible student or passing motorist notify the authorities.
- Keep students on the bus unless there is extensive damage or danger of further injury or fire.
- If another vehicle is involved, get the
    - driver's name, address, phone number, driver's license number, insurance company name and policy number
    - vehicle's license plate number and the state and the type of vehicle
    - name, address and phone number of witnesses or other drivers involved in the crash.

Break downs
- Turn on the emergency four-way hazard lights.
- Set out flares or reflectors.

    Keep the students on the bus until other transportation arrives unless there is danger of injury

Transporting Passengers

You must have a commercial driver's license if you plan to drive a vehicle that seats more than 15 persons, including the driver. You must also have a passenger endorsement on your CDL. To get the endorsement, you must pass:
- the written general knowledge exam;
- the written passenger bus exam
- the written air brakes exam if your vehicle is equipped with air brakes;
- the skills test required for the class of vehicle that you plan to drive.

Pre-trip inspection

Before driving your bus, make sure it is safe:
- Review the inspection report made by the previous driver.
- Sign the previous driver's report only if the defects reported earlier have been certified as repaired or certified as not needing repair. By signing this report, you certify that the defects reported earlier have been fixed.
- Conduct a pre-trip inspection.
- Follow the inspection method outlined in the General Knowledge portion of the CDL.

Also check:
- Access doors and panels: Close any emergency exits that are open as well as access panels (for baggage, restroom service, engine, etc.) before driving.
- Bus Interior:
    o Aisles and stairwells should always be clear.
    o Be sure that handholds and railings, floor covering, signaling devices (including the restroom emergency buzzer) and emergency exit handles are in good working order.
    o Be sure that all seats are securely fastened to the bus.
    o Never drive with an open emergency exit door or window.
    o The emergency exit sign on an emergency door must work. If the door has a red emergency light, the light must work. Turn it on at night and whenever you use your outside lights.
- Roof hatches: You may lock some emergency roof hatches in a partly open position for fresh air. However, do not leave them open all the time. Remember that the bus will have a higher clearance when the hatches are open.
- Safety equipment: Be sure your bus has a fire extinguisher and emergency reflectors as required by law. The bus must also have spare electrical fuses unless equipped with circuit breakers.

Always fasten your safety belt when you drive.

Loading the bus

Secure all baggage and freight so that:
- You can move freely and easily;
- Riders sitting by any window or door can exit in an emergency;
- Riders will not be injured if carry-ons fall or shift;
- All aisles and doorways are clear. Folding aisle seats are not allowed.

Watch for cargo or baggage containing hazardous materials. Hazardous materials pose a risk to health, safety and property. Most hazardous materials cannot be carried on a bus. Federal regulations require shippers to mark containers of hazardous materials with the materials name, ID number and hazard label. There are nine different hazard labels. The labels are four-inches and diamond-shaped. Do not transport hazardous materials unless you are sure federal regulations allow it. Buses may carry:

- Small-arms ammunition labeled ORM-D
- Emergency hospital supplies and drugs

Buses may never carry:

- Class 2 poison, liquid Class 6 poison, tear gas or irritating material
- More than 100 pounds of sold Class 6 poisons
- Explosives in the space occupied by people, except small arms ammunition
- Labeled radioactive materials in the space occupied by people
- More than 500 pounds total of allowed hazardous materials and no more than 100 pounds of any one class

Riders may sometimes board a bus carrying an unlabeled hazardous material. Do not allow riders to carry on common hazards such as car batteries or gasoline. Do not allow riders to stand forward of the rear of the driver's seat. Buses designed to allow standing must have a 2 inch line on the floor or some other marking that shows riders where they cannot stand. This is called the standee line. All standing riders must stay behind it.

Safe Driving with Buses

Passenger supervision

Many charter and intercity carriers have passenger comfort and safety rules. Mention rules about smoking, drinking and use of radio and tape players at the start of the trip. Explaining the rules at the beginning could help avoid trouble later on. Charter bus drivers should not allow passengers on the bus until departure time. While driving, scan the interior of your bus, as well as the road ahead. You may need to remind riders to keep their arms and heads inside the bus. Occasionally, you may have a drunk or disruptive rider. You must ensure this rider's safety as well as the safety of others. Don't discharge disruptive riders where it would be unsafe for them. It may be safer to wait until you reach the next scheduled stop or well-lighted area where there are other people. Many carriers have guidelines for handling disruptive riders. When you stop the bus, announce the location, reason for stopping, departure time and bus number. Caution riders to watch their step when leaving the bus. Wait for riders to sit down or brace themselves before starting the bus. Starting and stopping should be as smooth as possible to avoid rider injury.

Avoiding accidents

Use caution at all intersections, even if a signal or stop sign controls the intersection. Bus crashes often happen at intersections. Remember the clearance your bus needs. Watch for poles and tree limbs when you stop. Know the size of the gap your bus needs to accelerate and merge with traffic. Never assume other drivers will brake to give you room when you signal or begin to pull out. Reduce speed on curves. Crashes on curves result from excessive speed. In good weather, the posted speed on a curve is safe for cars, but may be too high for buses. If your bus leans toward the outside on a banked curve, you are driving too fast. Stop at railroad crossings:
- Stop your bus between 15 and 50 feet before railroad crossings.
- Listen and look in both directions for trains.
- Improve your ability to see or hear an approaching train by opening your forward door.
- If a train has just passed, make sure that another train isn't coming from the opposite direction.
- If your bus has a manual transmission, never change gears while crossing the tracks.

Slow down and check for other vehicles at:
- Street car crossings
- Railroad tracks used only for industrial switching within a business district
- Where a policeman or flagman is directing traffic
- If a traffic signal shows green
- At crossings marked "exempt" or abandoned."

Stop at drawbridges that do not have a signal light or traffic control attendant.
- Stop at least 50 feet before the draw of the bridge.
- Make sure the draw is completely closed before crossing.

Slow down at drawbridges that show a green traffic light or that have an attendant that controls traffic when the bridge opens.

After-trip vehicle inspection

Inspect your bus at the end of each shift. If you work for an interstate carrier, you must complete a written inspection report for each bus driven. The report must specify each bus and list any defect that would affect safety or result in a breakdown. The report must also state if there are no defects. Report damage to hand-holds, seat, emergency exits and windows at the end of your shift. Mechanics can make repairs before the bus goes out again. Mass transit drivers should also make sure passenger signaling devices and brake-door interlocks work properly.

Prohibited practices

Avoid fueling your bus with riders on board unless absolute necessary. Never refuel the bus in a closed building with riders on board. Don't talk with riders or engage in distracting activity while driving. Do not tow or push a disabled bus with riders on board unless getting off would be unsafe. Tow or push the bus to the nearest safe spot to discharge passengers. Follow your employer's guidelines on towing or pushing disabled buses.

Urban transit coaches may have a brake and accelerator interlock system. The interlock applies the brakes and holds the throttle in idle position when the rear door is open. The interlock releases when you close the rear door. Do not use this safety feature in place of the parking brake.

Passenger and School Bus Endorsement Tests

Part One

1. How do you certify corrected defects on your pre-trip inspection?
    a. Skip these items on your pre-trip inspection.
    b. Sign the previous driver report.
    c. Assume that the shop has handled these items.

2. During a pre-trip inspection what are some items that you must check?
    a. The standee line.
    b. The service brakes - parking brake - steering - lights - reflectors - tires.
    c. The number of bandages in first aid kits.

3. On which wheels may buses have recapped or regrooved tires?
    a. On all wheels.
    b. On all wheels except the front wheels
    c. On all wheels except the drivers.

4. What are three items of emergency equipment you must have on a bus?
    a. A fire extinguisher and a first aid kit and tire irons.
    b. Reflectors and stretchers and hydraulic jacks.
    c. Reflectors and a fire extinguisher and spare electric fuses.

5. Before driving who must inspect the emergency equipment?
    a. The shop.
    b. The driver.
    c. The dispatcher.

6. It is illegal to transport passengers if you have consumed?
    a. An intoxicating beverage within two hours.
    b. An intoxicating beverage within four hours.
    c. An intoxicating beverage within eight hours.

7. May passengers leave carry-on baggage in a doorway or in the aisle?
    a. Yes, unless there is a printed notice prohibiting it.
    b. No, unless no other space is available.
    c. No, There should be nothing in a doorway or the aisle that might trip riders.

8. What shape are hazardous material labels?
    a. Diamond-shaped.
    b. Round.
    c. Rectangular.

9. What is the maximum weight of hazardous materials allowed on a bus?
    a. One hundred pounds.
    b. Five hundred pounds.
    c. One thousand pounds.

10. What is the total weight of hazardous materials of one class allowed on a bus?
    a. One hundred pounds.
    b. Five hundred pounds.
    c. One thousand pounds.

Part Two

1. Can oxygen be carried on board by a passenger?
   a. No, gases are not permitted on board.
   b. Yes, if special written permission is received from the DOT.
   c. Yes, if medically prescribed for and in the possession of a passenger.

2. Can tear gas be transported on a bus?
   a. No, irritating material may not be carried.
   b. Yes, if written permission is received from the DOT
   c. Yes, if the containers meet certain packaging requirements.

3. Which of these two items can be carried on a bus by a rider?
   a. Car batteries.
   b. Gasoline.
   c. Neither one.

4. Where must passengers who are standing remain while the bus is underway?
   a. On buses where permitted they must stand at the back of the bus.
   b. On buses where permitted they must stand behind the standee line.
   c. Passengers are never allowed to stand on buses.

5. Can the emergency exit door be opened when the bus is underway?
   a. Never drive with an open emergency exit door.
   b. The emergency exit door must be open.
   c. The emergency exit door will be opened whenever the bus is stopped.

6. If you should discharge an unruly passenger, where should this be done?
   a. Within the city limits of an incorporated city.
   b. Only at a bus terminal.
   c. At a place that is safe for them.

7. Where else should you look while driving besides the road ahead?
   a. Also scan the emergency exit door every few seconds
   b. Also scan the emergency equipment to make sure that it is in place.
   c. Also scan the interior of the bus.

8. Can looking ahead prevent accidents with cars going in same direction?
   a. You can see changes in the traffic flow early enough to make adjustments
   b. You can see objects that are far away better than those that are close.
   c. You can see where passengers are waiting for your bus in time to stop.

9. If you have to move quickly to avoid an accident you want to know?
   a. Whether all of your passengers are wearing seat belts.
   b. Where your passengers are seated.
   c. Where other vehicles are around your bus.

10. Which can cause the most dangerous driving condition in poor weather?
    a. Rain.
    b. Ice.
    c. Snow.

Part Three

1. What is a factor that most affects the amount of traction that your bus has?
    a. The width of the road.
    b. The type and condition of the road surface.
    c. The brand name of your tires.

2. In backing up which is more dangerous?
    a. Backing to the left.
    b. Backing to the right
    c. They are equally dangerous.

3. One rule says that you should have how much following distance?
    a. At least three seconds.
    b. At least four seconds
    c. At least five seconds.

4. When braking, when will a bus have the most traction?
    a. When the wheels are rolling just short of locking up.
    b. During a skid.
    c. When the wheels have locked up.

5. When driving down a steep hill which is best?
    a. Shift down to a lower gear and not use your brakes.
    b. Shift down to a lower gear so that you will not use your brakes hard.
    c. Use your brakes only.

6. If a posted speed is 45 MPH what is a safe speed for your bus?
    a. It may be 45 miles per hour or it could be more.
    b. It will be exactly 45 miles per hour
    c. It may be 45 miles per hour or it could be less.

7. Which way will a bus lean if you are driving too fast on a banked curve?
    a. It will lean toward the inside
    b. It will lean in the direction of the turn.
    c. It will lean toward the outside.

8. What should you do about speed if the road becomes slippery?
    a. Reduce your speed gradually.
    b. Reduce your speed quickly.
    c. Stop immediately wherever you are.

9. Chains are required to be installed on which wheels?
    a. The front wheels
    b. The drive wheels.
    c. The back wheels of a tandem.

10. When may a disabled bus be towed to a safe place with passengers on board?
    a. When the emergency exit is not working.
    b. Only if getting off the bus would be inconvenient for the passengers.
    c. Only if getting off the bus would be unsafe for the passengers.

Part Four

1. Are you allowed to shift gears when crossing railroad tracks?
   a. Yes.
   b. No.
   c. Only when the crossing has been marked exempt.

2. How many feet away must you stop your bus for railroad tracks?
   a. At least 10 feet but not more than 50 feet from the crossing.
   b. At least 15 feet from the crossing.
   c. At least 15 feet but no more than 50 feet from the crossing.

3. You are stopped for a railroad crossing. When may you open your doors?
   a. You should open your forward door if that helps you see and hear.
   b. Never.
   c. You may open your emergency doors if it improves your view of the train.

4. How far must you stop from the draw of a drawbridge?
   a. At least 15 feet
   b. At least 25 feet.
   c. At least 50 feet.

5. Name a situation where you must not allow your bus to be fueled.
   a. When the air temperature is below freezing.
   b. When the engine is turned off and the driver is absent.
   c. When in a closed building with riders on board.

6. Interstate what kind of report must you complete at the end of your shift?
   a. You must complete a logbook page for each bus driven.
   b. You must make a list of the names of all passengers transported.
   c. You must complete a written inspection report for each bus driven.

7. Why should a driver count the number of students getting on a school bus?
   a. Helps to know if the bus is overloaded.
   b. Helps to determine if some passengers will have to stand.
   c. Helps to know if everyone is on the bus or is safely away from it.

8. Why is smooth handling of transmission and clutch a safety factor on busses?
   a. Smooth handling always reduces driver fatigue.
   b. Quick stops or sharp turns can cause injuries to passengers.
   c. Both of the above.

9. Which of the following can be stowed in the aisle on a school bus?
   a. Book bags and calculators and books.
   b. Lunches and coats and jackets.
   c. None of these.

10. Students planning to get off the school bus should not get up from their seat until?
    a. The school bus driver has turned on the flashing red lights.
    b. The bus has come to a complete stop.
    c. The driver tells them to get up.

Part Five

1. You should never bring your bus into the stop to pick up students until?
    a. There is no traffic in the area.
    b. A parent is present.
    c. The students have lined up properly.

2. What should you do before the students are allowed to start toward the bus?
    a. The bus should be stopped and the door should be opened.
    b. The students should have seen your bus and are aware that it is approaching.
    c. You should be slowing down approaching the bus stop.

3. Why should you always count the number of students waiting for your approaching bus?
    a. The school receives state moneys based upon the number of students.
    b. You will know when everyone has boarded the bus or gotten safely away from it.
    c. You are required to make written reports.

4. Buses parked in line at the school should be parked so that?
    a. Evacuation drills can be held that utilize the front and back exits.
    b. Students will not have to walk very far between their classroom and the bus.
    c. No one can walk between the busses.

5. You must know the student loading areas on your school bus route because?
    a. You load or unload passengers only in designated areas.
    b. Loading and unloading areas are not allowed near railroad tracks.
    c. Both of these.

6. Students who have to cross the road after leaving the bus should walk?
    a. Behind the bus only.
    b. Far enough in front of the bus so that the driver can see them.
    c. In front of the bus but as close to the bus as possible.

7. Usually the best position for a bus when students are crossing the road is?
    a. On the left side of the road.
    b. On the right edge of the roadway.
    c. In the middle of the road.

8. What is the only real control that you have over students leaving the school bus?
    a. Turning off the engine.
    b. Opening the door.
    c. Threatening them with punishment.

9. Employees using drugs and alcohol have how many times as many accidents as unencumbered employees?
    a. Twice as many.
    b. Three to four times as many.
    c. Five times as many.

10. Which will make you tire earlier?
    a. You do not like what you are doing.
    b. You have exercised beforehand.
    c. You are hungry.

Part Six

1. What should you do when driving for a long period?
   a. Keep the window rolled down.
   b. Take regular breaks.
   c. Drink coffee.

2. Which of these can fully recharge the body?
   a. Coffee and stretching your legs.
   b. Just coffee.
   c. None of these.

3. Should you start to pass another vehicle before a no-passing zone?
   a. Yes, if you begin your pass before you reach the solid yellow lines.
   b. Only if the pass can be completed safely before the no-passing zone.
   c. Yes, if no oncoming traffic is coming.

4. On a two-lane road can you pass a car that is passing another vehicle?
   a. Yes.
   b. Yes, only if the person knows you are passing them.
   c. No.

5. Why must you be careful when passing a heavy vehicle going downhill?
   a. The other driver cannot see you as easily as he can when going uphill.
   b. The heavy vehicle may be picking up speed.
   c. It is illegal to pass a vehicle going downhill.

6. Why is it harder to pass at night?
   a. You cannot judge distance as well because of oncoming headlights.
   b. Your own headlights do not give you enough light to pass.
   c. Other drivers cannot see you at night.

7. When passing a vehicle at night what is important to remember?
   a. Have your highbeams on.
   b. Use your lowbeams.
   c. Flash your lights.

8. Before passing many drivers make the mistake of?
   a. Following too far behind.
   b. Following too closely.
   c. Turning their blinker on too soon.

9. Where should you check before passing?
   a. Check only what is in front of you.
   b. Check only what is to the side of you.
   c. Check in your mirrors and over your shoulder and behind you.

10. Why should you be aware of a car in front of a car you will be passing?
    a. It may try to pass also.
    b. It might get a flat tire.
    c. To be sure you can safely return to your lane after completing the pass.

Part Seven

1. Why does it require more time for the eyes to adjust at night?
    a. There is less light at night.
    b. Different parts of the eyes are used.
    c. Both of the above.

2. When are drivers more likely to be tired?
    a. When they first get up in the morning.
    b. After lunch.
    c. At night.

3. What may be the only notice that drivers following you have at night?
    a. Your taillights.
    b. Your back bumper.
    c. Your rear window.

4. When can your rear view mirrors be a handicap to you at night?
    a. When they make other objects seem closer than they are.
    b. When the glare of other headlights in them blinds you.
    c. When they do not show your blind spots.

5. If you are trying to avoid the glare of oncoming headlights you?
    a. Are looking to the right edge of the road and could miss tinted windshields.
    b. Are looking to the right edge of the road and could miss fog lights.
    c. Are looking to the right edge of the road and could miss a threat from the left.

6. Which of the following is much harder to judge at night?
    a. The time.
    b. Your strength.
    c. Distance.

7. Should you cross over to the far left lane as soon as you enter a freeway?
    a. Yes as long as you are careful.
    b. No work over to the left lane when it is safe to do so.
    c. Yes but if you have an accident it is your fault.

8. What should you do if you miss your freeway off ramp?
    a. Put the vehicle in reverse and go back to the off ramp.
    b. Cross over the median and make a U-turn.
    c. Take the next off ramp.

9. When you are on the freeway - if you can do so safely maintain a speed?
    a. That is the average of other drivers.
    b. That is slower than the other drivers.
    c. That is faster than the other drivers.

10. Why is it important to keep a safe following distance on the freeway?
    a. So you will not get a ticket for tailgating.
    b. So you can adjust quickly if traffic comes to a complete stop.
    c. So you will save fuel.

Part Eight

1. When can you park on the freeway?
   a. When you need to stop to look at a map.
   b. When you need to get out and stretch your legs.
   c. Only in emergencies.

2. If red is reflected back from pavement markings you are going?
   a. In the right direction on the freeway.
   b. To be coming to the end of the freeway.
   c. In the wrong direction on the freeway.

3. When entering the freeway your best strategy is to?
   a. Try to keep your speed low.
   b. Merge at or close to the speed of traffic on the freeway.
   c. Stop until there is a spot to enter.

4. When preparing to turn left, how should you keep your wheels pointing?
   a. To the left.
   b. To the right.
   c. Straight ahead

5. What is the best tactic to use before crossing an intersection?
   a. Look right - then left - then right again.
   b. Look left - then right - then left again.
   c. Look to the rear - then ahead and then to the rear again.

6. What is a yield sign?
   a. A yield sign tells you to stop.
   b. A yield sign tells you to slow down and be ready to stop.
   c. A yield sign tells you to slow down to ten miles per hour.

7. How should an intersection with flashing red lights be treated?
   a. As if it was controlled by stop signs.
   b. As if it was a two-way intersection.
   c. No special treatment must be given to the intersection.

8. The light turns green and as the car ahead starts forward you?
   a. Wait a moment so that you will have a safe following distance.
   b. Proceed as closely as possible behind that car.
   c. Stop at the limit line to make sure it is safe.

9. How does failing to look far enough in front of you affect your driving?
   a. It can cause your vehicle to weave in and out.
   b. It can cause you to stop too smoothly.
   c. It can cause you to be in the wrong gear.

10. Why is it often difficult to look far enough ahead when driving at night?
   a. There is too much light inside your vehicle.
   b. The glare from oncoming headlights may force you to look to the shoulder.
   c. The pavement tends to be drier and shines more at night.

Part Nine

1. At night your ability to steer a vehicle is reduced because?
    a. You cannot see as well.
    b. You may not be able to look down the road far enough.
    c. Both of the above.

2. Since you must know what is in front of you how should you use your eyes?
    a. You should be gazing straight ahead at all times.
    b. You should either be looking at your dashboard or looking straight ahead.
    c. You should be shifting your view every few seconds.

3. How often should you look in your rear view mirrors?
    a. Several times per minute.
    b. Only when you are changing lanes or backing up.
    c. Once a minute.

4. What is a warning that you are getting tired?
    a. You are watching out for everything around you.
    b. You are beginning to look in one place too long.
    c. Both of the above.

5. Can your ability to look around you be handicapped by what you see?
    a. No, you will continue to keep your eyes moving at all times.
    b. No, you are only interested in the vehicles that could be a threat to you.
    c. Yes, certain things will attract your attention more than others.

6. A vehicle that is straddling lanes is a possible sign of a drunk driver?
    a. Yes.
    b. Yes, only if it is at night.
    c. No.

7. Is it OK to have a drink if you are still under the maximum allowed?
    a. Yes, because you are not legally drunk.
    b. Yes, because you are still able to drive.
    c. No, because you do not know you can drive safely.

8. What type of drug is alcohol?
    a. A stimulant.
    b. A depressant.
    c. An opiate.

9. How is your reaction time affected by alcohol?
    a. It is speeded up.
    b. It stays the same.
    c. It slows down.

10. Can your performance be affected the day after you have been drinking?
    a. Yes.
    b. No.
    c. Only if you drank a large amount.

Answer Key

Part One

1. B: Sign the previous driver report.
2. B: The service brakes - parking brake - steering - lights - reflectors - tires.
3. B: On all wheels except the front wheels
4. C: Reflectors and a fire extinguisher and spare electric fuses.
5. B: The driver.
6. B: An intoxicating beverage within four hours.
7. C: No, There should be nothing in a doorway or the aisle that might trip riders.
8. A: Diamond-shaped.
9. B: Five hundred pounds.
10. A: One hundred pounds.

Part Two

1. C: Yes, if medically prescribed for and in the possession of a passenger.
2. A: No, irritating material may not be carried.
3. C: Neither one.
4. B: On buses where permitted, they must stand behind the standee line.
5. A: Never drive with an open emergency exit door.
6. C: At a place that is safe for them.
7. C: Also scan the interior of the bus.
8. A: You can see changes in the traffic flow early enough to make adjustments
9. C: Where other vehicles are around your bus.
10. B: Ice.

Part Three

1. B: The type and condition of the road surface.
2. B: Backing to the right
3. B: At least four seconds
4. A: When the wheels are rolling just short of locking up.
5. B: Shift down to a lower gear so that you will not use your brakes hard.
6. C: It may be 45 miles per hour or it could be less.
7. C: It will lean toward the outside.
8. A: Reduce your speed gradually.
9. B: The drive wheels.
10. C: Only if getting off the bus would be unsafe for the passengers.

Part Four

1. B: No.
2. C: At least 15 feet but no more than 50 feet from the crossing.
3. A: You should open your forward door if that helps you see and hear.
4. C: At least 50 feet.
5. C: When in a closed building with riders on board.
6. C: You must complete a written inspection report for each bus driven.
7. C: Helps to know if everyone is on the bus or is safely away from it.
8. B: Quick stops or sharp turns can cause injuries to passengers.
9. C: None of these.
10. B: The bus has come to a complete stop.

Part Five

1. C: The students have lined up properly.
2. A: The bus should be stopped and the door should be opened.
3. B: You will know when everyone has boarded the bus or gotten safely away from it.
4. C: No one can walk between the busses.
5. C: Both of these.
6. B: Far enough in front of the bus so that the driver can see them.
7. B: On the right edge of the roadway.
8. B: Opening the door.
9. B: Three to four times as many.
10. A: You do not like what you are doing.

Part Six

1. B: Take regular breaks.
2. C: None of these.
3. B: Only if the pass can be completed safely before the no-passing zone.
4. C: No.
5. B: The heavy vehicle may be picking up speed.
6. A: You cannot judge distance as well because of oncoming headlights.
7. B: Use your lowbeams.
8. B: Following too closely.
9. C: Check in your mirrors and over your shoulder and behind you.
10. C: To be sure you can safely return to your lane after completing the pass.

Part Seven

1. C: Both of the above.
2. C: At night.
3. A: Your taillights.
4. B: When the glare of other headlights in them blinds you.
5. C: Are looking to the right edge of the road and could miss a threat from the left.
6. C: Distance.
7. B: No work over to the left lane when it is safe to do so.
8. C: Take the next off ramp.
9. A: That is the average of other drivers.
10. B: So you can adjust quickly if traffic comes to a complete stop.

Part Eight

1. C: Only in emergencies.
2. C: In the wrong direction on the freeway.
3. B: Merge at or close to the speed of traffic on the freeway.
4. C: Straight ahead
5. B: Look left - then right - then left again.
6. B: A yield sign tells you to slow down and be ready to stop.
7. A: As if it was controlled by stop signs.
8. A: Wait a moment so that you will have a safe following distance.
9. A: It can cause your vehicle to weave in and out.
10. B: The glare from oncoming headlights may force you to look to the shoulder.

Part Nine

1. C: Both of the above.
2. C: You should be shifting your view every few seconds.
3. A: Several times per minute.
4. B: You are beginning to look in one place too long.
5. C: Yes, certain things will attract your attention more than others.
6. A: Yes.
7. C: No, because you do not know you can drive safely.
8. B: A depressant.
9. C: It slows down.
10. A: Yes.

Made in the USA
Middletown, DE
20 November 2015